The World's Greatest
Love Story

Reverend J.A. Jefferson

authorHOUSE®

HOW THE WORLD'S GREATEST LOVE STORY CAME TO US

In reading the Bible I learned about how the Bible was put together, how to be strengthened with and by the Spirit in the inner man; that Christ may dwell in a person's heart by faith, and that He is rooted and grounded in love. It is well known as the World's Greatest Book of Love.

THE OLD TESTAMENT
It brings with it the law and the sacred writings of Moses which make up the first five books of the Old Testament. These were read aloud in their entirety to the Israelites every seven years. Copies were kept with care and reverence in the Ark of the Covenant in the Tabernacle, and preserved in the Temple. They were in Hebrew, except for brief parts of Ezra and Daniel and one short passage in Jeremiah which are in Aramaic. Aramaic took the place of Hebrew after the captivity in Babylon and was the language used in daily life by Jesus and the disciples.

THE NEW TESTAMENT
The books of the New Testament were written in a century. They were written by men who, for the most part, came from lowly walks of life, as we can see in the everyday life of the said religious leaders, but the distinction of giving inspired account of the life of Jesus and expounding on Jesus' teachings.

Although the disciples of Jesus spoke Aramaic, they also spoke Greek, which was the commercial language throughout much of the Roman Empire. In was a Kline or common Greek and in this language the New Testament was first written. This is how the world's greatest love story came to us.

By studying and reading both the Old and New Testaments we discover God's purpose and affirmation of His great love for His people. It was because of His great love for us that He sent His Son, a gift we have no means to deserve. John 3:16 tells the story: *For God so loved the world, that He gave His only begotten Son, that whoever believes in Him should not perish, but have everlasting life.*

HAVE FAITH AND BELIEVE

BIBLE STUDY GUIDE: The World's Greatest Love Story

AuthorHouse™
1663 Liberty Drive
Bloomington, IN 47403
www.authorhouse.com
Phone: 1 (800) 839-8640

Published by AuthorHouse 12/07/2015

ISBN: 978-1-4969-3664-6 (sc)
ISBN: 978-1-4969-3663-9 (e)

Print information available on the last page.

This book is printed on acid-free paper.

THE WORLD'S GREATEST LOVE STORY
PERTAINING TO THE OLD AND NEW TESTAMENT
Translation of the original tongue and with the former referenced translations diligently compared and reviewed. Quotations are from the Authorized or the King James Version of the Bible.

Reverend J. A. Jefferson
E-mail: JJ2558@bellsouth.net
WEBSITE www.chaplainjefferson.com
1-864-338-8552

ABOUT THE AUTHOR

The author has studied the Bible from the time he was solemnly and publicly set apart in 1985 and ordained to the work of the gospel ministry by the authority and order of the Sixteenth Street Baptist Church under Reverend Curtis Kyle. He was publicly ordained in 1990 to the work of the Gospel Ministry to the views of the Holy Bible and the Christian Faith of the Pentecostal Church.

The author received instruction in Part I and II of the Old and New Testament at Howard University in 1977. He was a member of the 1988 Ministry Class at the Jericho Christian Training Center, Washington, DC; attended Chaplain Moral Leadership Staff College at Dover College, Dover, Delaware in 1988; then completed further studies in Moral Leadership at the Middle East Region Chaplain's Staff College at Dover Air Force Base, Dover,  Maryland in 2000. That same year he received the Chaplain of the Year Award.

After serving as chaplain for the District of Columbia Jail, the author became chaplain for the District of Columbia Department of Corrections under the federal government from 1997 until 2004. He joined the Chaplain Department at the District of Columbia General Hospital in 1985 and served diligently until his retirement in 2004. He also served as police Clergy with the Philadelphia

Police Department and for 9 years volunteered as a Big Brother in the District of Columbia.

Chaplain John A. Jefferson

E-MAIL: jj2558@bellsouth.net

WEBSITE www.chaplainjefferson.com

PREFACE

OVERVIEW

The components of this book will enhance the reader's spiritual growth in the biblical ethics by placing these principles at the fingertips of the reader's wealth of related information from which to draw.

Reading and studying this bible study guide will enhance your Christian walk as well as your growth in faith. It will give the biblical way of living based on its ethical principles and presents God's plan for salvation and daily Christian living. I pray that the annotating study of this Bible Study Guide will bless your spiritual life and growth for years to come.

DOCTRINAL FOOTNOTES

These notes provide a system for studying the doctrines of the Bible and for teaching them through the Scripture. By reading the notes within one topic area, you will complete a total survey of that particular Bible teaching with its explanations, illustrations, and practical applications for daily living. The comprehensive introductions, outlines, and reflection worksheets will give you an opportunity to strengthen your understanding of each topic.

REFLECTION

<u>Purpose</u>. This book is a very good teaching tool which emphasizes the biblical ethics and the principles of Bible Teaching. This purpose of this book is to provide a better understanding of the one God, his love for us, and why He calls to each of us. This Bible study guide explains God's purpose and his charter to His people who He loved so much that He gave his only begotten Son. He called and created us for His glory, and only through Him do we have salvation and eternal life. This book is also intended to show how God provides spiritual strength to His followers and increases that strength so we will not become faint and weary. *They shall mount up with the wings as eagles; they shall run and not be weary; they shall walk and not faint* (Isaiah 40:31).

The world's greatest love story is the exciting and dramatic story of the life of Jesus and his message to each of us. The twofold designation "Jesus Christ" combines the personal name "Jesus" and the title "Christ" that mean "Anointed" or "Messiah." His birth and early years in Bethlehem and Nazareth are followed by the story of his baptism, ministry, and message to us.

<u>Willingness to Serve</u> (John 21:15-17). Jesus asked, **Do you love me more than these**? The answer, *Yes*, expressed the strong inspirational love of Simon Peter for Jesus. *Yes Lord; you know that I love you. Then Jesus said unto him, **feed by lambs*** (John 21:15). Jesus is asking you, **Do you love me?** When you have the right attitude of the ethical teaching of Jesus Christ you will display the right attitude of love and not the emotional kind of love that does not always last. Jesus wants your lasting love (phileo love) signifies affection and also results in emotional love. I like to believe this was the reason Jesus asked Peter three times if he loved Jesus, because He wanted Peter to be sure. Jesus knew how much Peter loved him but wanted Peter to know the depth of his love for Jesus. Was he willing to die for Jesus just as Jesus loved us enough to die for us (sacrificial love).

Jesus has a way of getting to the heart of any matter. We will discover in John 21:15-17 how Peter faced his true feelings. Today we don't have the physical Jesus next to us who loves us but we serve God through Jesus Christ by faith and the example Jesus gave us for loving and treating others.

It is God's nature to love. God sent His only Son into the world to die for it (John 3:16; Romans 5:8). When you read this book you will have a better understanding about love. I have taken the time by the grace of God through our Lord Jesus Christ to read and study His Word then share the understanding God has given me through the Holy Spirit. It has been a blessing to me to have been able to do this so that you may also have a better understanding of God's holy word. May God bless and keep you. Amen

TABLE OF CONTENTS

CHAPTER 2. MAN'S RELATIONSHIP WITH GOD 31

CHAPTER 3. THE LIFE OF JESUS CHRIST 48

INTRODUCTION

THE WORLD'S GREATEST LOVE STORY

This story is about a loving God who gave His only begotten Son to show how much He loved His people. He sent His Son into a sick and dying world to save them from their sin which justified them for death eternal.

The focus is on the love the Son had for His Father. The Son proved His love and was continually obedient to the Father's will. This kind of love is not self-centered. It reaches out into the world and draws others into the loving household of His Father.

The pattern of love between Father and Son and their love for others set the basis for all love relationships. Is your love relationship for others based on this kind of selfless love? Are you willing to give freely to the point of self-sacrifice for others?

This is what we do when we love our heavenly Father. If you claim the heavenly Father as your Father, are you being obedient to Him just as His Son was? Are you willing to give your life to glorify the Father and the Son?

So much that He was willing to give His life to please His Father even to the point of His being glorified in the Son. The Father paid dearly with the gift of His Son's life, the highest price He could pay to show how much He loved us. What are you willing to do to show how much you love your heavenly Father? Is it enough to show others who hate you and don't have anything to do with you? Do you show them that you love them anyway?

THE BOOK OF JOHN CONCERNING THE SON OF GOD

- <u>Purpose</u>: To prove conclusively that Jesus is the Son of God and that all who believe in him will have eternal life.

- <u>Author</u>: John the apostle, son of Zebedee, brother of James, called a "Son of Thunder."

- <u>To Whom Written</u>: New Christians and searching non-Christians.

- <u>Date Written</u>: Probably A.D. 85-90.

- <u>Setting</u>: Written after the destruction of Jerusalem in A.D. 70 and before John's exile to the island of Pathos.

- <u>Key Verse</u>: *Jesus did many other miraculous signs in the presence of his disciples, which are not recorded in this book. These are written that you may believe that Jesus is the Christ, the Son of God, and that by believing you may have life in his name* (John 20:30-31).

- <u>Key People</u>: Jesus, John the Baptist, the disciples, Mary, Martha, Lazarus, Jesus' mother, Pilate, Mary Magdalene.

- <u>Key Place</u>: Judean countryside, Samaria, Galilee, Bethany, Jerusalem.

- <u>Special Features</u>: Of the eight miracles recorded, six are unique among the Gospels to John, as is the "Upper Room Discourse" (John 14:14). Over 90 percent of John is unique to his Gospel. According to the study John does not contain a genealogy or any record of Jesus' birth, childhood, temptation, transfiguration, appointment of the disciples, nor any account of Jesus' parables, ascension, or Great Commission. This is a study of the life and teachings of Jesus, not much is found on his childhood life.

COMPARISON OF THE FOUR GOSPELS

All four gospels present the life and teachings of Jesus. Each book focuses on a unique facet of Jesus and his character.

	MATTHEW	MARK	LUKE	JOHN
Jesus is . . .	The Promised King	The Servant Of God	The Son of Man	The Son of God
The original readers were . . .	Jews	Gentiles, Romans	Greeks	Christians
Significant themes . . .	Jesus is Messiah because He fulfilled Testament Prophecy	Jesus backed up His words with His actions	Jesus was God but also fully human	Jesus is required for salvation
Character of the writer . . .	Teacher	Storyteller	Historian	Theologian
Emphasis on . . .	Jesus' sermons and words	Jesus' miracles and actions	Jesus' humanity	The principles of Jesus' teaching

CHAPTER 1. LOVE

1. YOU ARE MY WTINESSES (ISAIAH 43:10)

<u>Difficulties of Life</u>. Going through difficulties in life will either cause you to drown or force you to grow stronger. If you go on your own strength, you are more likely to drown. If you invite the Lord to go with you, He will protect you.

But now thus said the Lord that created you, O Jacob, and He that formed you, O Israel, fear not: for I have redeemed you; I have called you by name; you are mine (Isaiah 32:1).

<u>Strength in the Lord</u>. Israel's task was to be a witness (Isaiah 44:8), telling the world who God is and what He has done. Believers today share the responsibility of being God's witnesses. Do people know what God is like through your words and example? They cannot see God directly, but they can see Him reflected in you.

You are my witnesses, said the Lord, and my servant whom I have chosen: that I am he: Before me there was no God formed, neither shall there be after me (Isaiah 43:10).

<u>Important Decisions</u>. When we have an important decision we sometimes think we can't trust anyone not even God. But God knows what is best for us. He is a better judge of what we need rather than want we want. We must trust Him completely in every choice we make. We should not omit careful thinking or belittle our God-given ability to reason; but we should not trust our own ideas to the exclusion of all others.

Trust in the Lord with all your heart; and lean not unto your own understanding (Proverbs 3:5).

2. GOD'S EXPECTATION OF US (ISAIAH 43:26)

<u>God's Expectations are Clear</u>. God has told us many different times and has shown us what favors He had bestowed upon us just as He did for Isaiah. He formed them for Himself just as He did us, intending that we should show forth His praise. But they had not done so; they had frustrated God's expectations from Him, and made every ill returned to Him for His favors.

This is what God said they had done. They had cast off prayer: they have not called upon me, O Jacob! Jacob was a man famous for prayer (Hosea 12:4).

<u>Allow God to Guide Us</u>. Receiving God's guidance, we must acknowledge God in all our ways. This means turning every area of life over to Him. About a thousand years later, Jesus emphasized this same truth (Matthew 6:33).

But seek you first the kingdom of God, and his righteousness; and all these things shall be added unto you (Matthew 6:33).

<u>Look at Our Values and Priorities</u>. What is important to you? In what areas of your life have you already acknowledge God? The areas where you attempt to restrict or ignore His influence will cause you grief.

In all your ways acknowledge him, and He shall direct your paths. Be not wise in your own eyes: fear the Lord, and depart from evil (Proverbs 3:7).

<u>Delight in the Lord</u>. David calls us to take delight in the Lord and to commit everything we have and do to Him. The question is: Do we do this? To delight in someone means to experience great pleasure and joy in his or her presence. This happens only when you know that person well. To delight in the Lord, we must know Him better.

Delight yourself in the Lord; and He shall give you the desires of your heart (Psalm 37:4)

3. FREEDOM FROM BURDENS (MATTHEW 11:28-30)

<u>Heavy Burdens</u>. A yoke is a heavy wooden harness that fits over the shoulders of an ox or oxen. It is attached to a piece of equipment the oxen are to pull. A person may be carrying heavy burdens of

- sin

- excessive demands of religious leaders (Matthew 23:4; Acts 15:10)

- oppression and persecution

- weariness in the search of God

<u>Jesus Frees Us from All Burdens</u>. The rest that Jesus promises is love, healing, and peace with God, not the end of all labor. A relationship with God changes meaningless, wearisome toil into spiritual productivity and purpose.

[28] Come unto me, all you that labor and are heavy laden, and I will give you rest. [29] Take my yoke upon you, and learn of me; for I am meek and lowly in heart: and you shall find rest unto your souls. [30] For my yoke is easy, and my burden is light (Matthew 11:28-30).

4. UNITY OF THE SPIRIT OF CHRIST (EPHESIANS 4)

The <u>Role of the Holy Spirit</u>. To build unity is one of the Holy Spirit's important roles. He leads, but we must be willing to be led and to do our part in keeping the peace. We do that by focusing on God and not on ourselves, as we discover in John's writing.

That which is born of the flesh is flesh; and that which is born of the Spirit is Spirit (John 3:6).

John truly baptized with water; but you shall be baptized with the Holy Ghost not many days hence (Acts 1:5; Ephesians 1:13,14).

United in One Body Under Christ. Corinthians talks about the body and its many members. All believers in Christ belong to one body. All are united under one head. Christ Himself is the head of the body (1-Corinthians 12:12-26). Each believer has God-given abilities that can strengthen the whole body. Your special ability may seem small or large, but it is yours to use in God's service. Ask God to use your unique gift to contribute to the strength and health of the body as a child of His.

God is Over All. This shows His overruling care (transcendence). He is through all and in all. This shows His active presence in the world and in the lives of believers (Immanence). Any view of God that violates either His transcendence or His immanence does not paint a picture of God. What we are talking about is the subjective of God which is His Word.

Endeavor to Keep the Unity of the Spirit (Ephesians 4: 3, 13). Endeavor to keep the unity of the Spirit in the bond of peace until we all come in the unity of the faith, and of the knowledge of the Son of God, unto a perfect man, unto the measure of the statue of the fullness of Christ.

Setting Aside Differences. Too often believers are separated because of minor differences in doctrine. The Bible shows those areas where Christians must agree to attain true unity. When believers have this unity of the Spirit petty differences should never be allowed to dissolve that unity.

5. IN THE BOND OF PEACE (EPHESIANS 4)

Spirit in the Bond of Peace: Endeavoring which is our duty to keep the unity of the spirit in the bond of peace (Ephesians 4:3).

The Gift of God through Christ: But unto every one of us is given grace according to the measure of the gift of Christ (Ephesians 4:7).

Gift of the Spirit: And He gave some, apostles; and some prophets; and some evangelists; and some pastors and teachers (Ephesians 4:11).

Edifying of the Body of Christ: For the perfecting of the saints, for the work of the ministry, for the edifying of the body of Christ (Ephesians 4:12).

Unity of Faith: Till we all come in the unity of the faith, and of the knowledge of the Spirit of God, unto a Perfect man, unto the measure of the stature of the fullness of Christ (Ephesians 4:13).

Carried Away by Every Wind: That we henceforth be no more children, tossed to and fro, and carried about with every wind of doctrine, by the sleight of men, and conning craftiness, whereby they lie in wait to deceive; (Ephesians 4:14).

Speaking the Truth: But speaking the truth in love, may grow up into Him in all things, which is the head, even Christ (Ephesians 4:15).

6. MAKING INCREASE OF THE BODY

Making Increase of the body: *From whom the whole body fitly joined together and compacted by that which every joint supply, according to the effectual working in the measure of every part, make increase of the body unto the edifying of itself in love* (Ephesians 4:16).

The Way to God is through Jesus. This is one of the most basic and important passages in the Scripture. How can we know the way to God? Only through Jesus because Jesus is the way because He is both God and man. There are some who don't believe this, but when you read and study the Bible you will learn this basic truth for yourself. By uniting our lives with His we are united with God. Trust Jesus to take you to the Father and all the benefits of being God's child will be yours.

Jesus said unto Him, **I am the way, the truth, And the life: no man comes unto the Father, But by me** (John 14:6).

The truth into which the Holy Spirit guides us is the truth about Christ. The Spirit also helps us through patient practice to discern right from wrong.

Howbeit it when he, the Spirit of truth, is come He will guide you into all truth: for He shall not speak of Himself, but whatsoever He shall hear, that shall He speak: and He will show you things to come (John 16:13).

7. BELIEVERS ARE ONE IN UNITY

As one our unity is experienced in:

Body:	The fellowship of believers the church
Spirit:	The Holy Spirit, who activates the fellowship
Hope:	That glorious future to which we are all called
Lord:	Christ, to whom we all belong
Faith:	Our singular commitment to Christ
Baptism:	Baptism the sign of entry into the church
God:	God, who is our Father who keeps us for eternity through Jesus Christ

8. UNCONDITIONAL LOVE

While all believers are sons and daughters of God, only Jesus lives in this special unique relationship. According to John 3:18, He *that believeth on Him is not condemned: but He that believeth not is condemned already, because he has not believeth in the name of the only begotten Son of God.*

John also wrote, *For God so loved the world; that He gave His only begotten Son, that whosoever believeth in Him should not perish, but have everlasting life* (John 3:16). This is about the love of God, which is what 1-John is showing and is all about.

Herein is love, not that we love God, but that He loved us, and sent His Son to be the propitiation for our sins (1-John 4: 10).

9. THE MOST REMARKABLE BOOK OF LOVE IN THE WORLD

Love is the highest esteem which God has for His human children and the highest regard which they, in return, should have for Him and each other. Because of the hundreds of references to love in the Bible, it is certainly the most remarkable book of love in the world. It records the greatest love story ever written. God proved His unconditional love for us when He sent His Son to die on the cross. *Herein is love, not because we love God, but because He loved us, and sent His Son to be the propitiation for our sins* (1-John 4:10).

<u>Love Explains Why God Creates</u>. Here are five things that explain why God creates.

(1) Why God creates..................................Because He loves, He creates people to love

(2) Why God cares...................................Because He loves them, He even cares for sinful people

(3) Why we are free to choose.................God wants a loving response from us

(4) Why Christ died. ....His love for us caused Him to seek a solution to the problem of sin

(5) Why we receive eternal life. ....God's love expresses itself to us forever.

Nothing sinful or evil can exist in God's presence. He is absolute-goodness. He cannot overlook, condone, or excuse sin as though it never happened. He loves us, but His love does not make Him morally lax. If we trust in Christ, we will not have to bear the penalty for our sins. We will be acquitted of our sins by His atoning sacrifice.

Christ Himself bore our sins in His body on the tree, so that we, being dead to sin, should live unto righteousness: by whose stripes we were healed (1-Peter 2:24).

Paul wrote, *Therefore as by the offence of one judgment came upon all men to condemnation; even so by the righteousness of one the free gift came upon all men unto justification of life* (Romans 5:18).

10. CHILDREN OF HEIRS (ROMANS 8:17)

Children of Heirs. What a promise this is to those who love Christ! We can reign over sin's power, over death's threats, and over Satan's attacks. Eternal life is ours now and forever. In the power and protection of Jesus Christ, we can overcome temptation.

Because in Christ we are the same to God through Christ because of being children of God, and if His children, then heirs of God, and joint-heirs with Christ Jesus; if it be that we suffer with Him, that we may be also glorified together (Romans 8: 17).

One of God's Attributes is Love. Love is not only one of God's attributes; it is also an essential part of His nature. "God is love." The Bible declares God's love in John's writings (1-John) in saying "God is love," not "Love is God." The shallow and selfish view of love in our world has turned these words around and contaminated our understanding of love.

The world thinks that love is what makes a person feel good and that it is all right in order to obtain such "love." But that isn't real love. Love is the exact opposite selfishness and God is not that kind of "love." Real love is like God who is holy, just, and perfect. If we truly know God, we will love as He does.

He that love not know not God; for God is love (1-John 4:8).

The Christ Revelation. In 1-John we read that the Christ revelation is what should endear it to us, the revelation of the divine love. The articles of our revealed faith are but so many articles relating to the divine love. The history of the loving Christ is the history of God's love to us. All His transactions in and with His Son were but justifications of His love to us, and that means to advance us to the love of God: *God was in Christ reconciling the world unto Himself* (2-Corinthians 5:16); 1-John says we know and believe the love that God has for us.

God is love; and He that dwell in love dwell in God, and God in Him (1-John 4:16).

11. PERSONIFICATION OF PERFECT LOVE

The Personification of Perfect Love. The personification of perfect love is such an outstanding artistic representation of a person that such love surpasses our powers of understanding. "The fullness of God" is fully expressed only in Christ (Colossians 2:9-10). For in Him dwells all the fullness of the Godhead bodily. And you are complete in Him, which is the head of all principality and power.

Union with Christ. We who believe and have Christ as our Lord are in union with Christ and through His empowering Spirit we are complete. We have all the fullness of God available to us, but we must appropriate that fullness through faith and through prayer as we daily live for Him.

The Holy Spirit. Paul's prayer for the Ephesians is also for you. You can ask the Holy Spirit to fill every aspect of your life to the fullest.

And to know the love of Christ, which passes knowledge, that you might be filled with all the fullness of God (Ephesians 3:19).

Paul Asserts Christ's deity. *In Christ all the fullness of the Deity lives in bodily form* which means that all of God was in Christ's human body. When we have Christ we have everything we need for salvation and right living. Read Colossians 1:15-16 for more on the divine nature of Christ. This is one of the strongest statements about the divine nature of Christ found anywhere in the Bible.

Jesus Reveals God. Jesus is not only equal to God (Philippians 2:6), He is God (John 10:30, 38; John 12:45; John 14:1-11). As the image of the invisible God, He is the exact representation of God. He not only reflects God, but He reveals God to us (John 1:18; 14:9). As the firstborn over all creation, He has all the priority and authority of the firstborn prince in a king's household.

Who is the image of the invisible God, the firstborn of every creature: for by Him were all things created that are in heaven and that are in earth, visible and invisible, whether they be thrones or dominions or principalities or power, all things were created by Him and for Him (Colossians 1:15-16).

12. CHRIST IS SUPREME

<u>The Central Truth of Christianity</u>. Christ is supreme over all creation including the spiritual world. Like the Colossian believers, we must believe in the deity of Jesus Christ and that Jesus is God or our Christian faith is hollow, misdirected, and meaningless. This is a central truth of Christianity. We must oppose those who say that Jesus was merely a prophet or a good teacher.

<u>Everlasting Love</u>. Love like this is everlasting. Because of God's kindness and deep and everlasting love, He reaches toward His people. He is eager to do the best for them and is waiting for them to let Him. After hearing many words of warning about sin, this reminder of God's magnificent love is refreshing. Do not dread things of God. Instead, you will see Him lovingly drawing us toward Himself if you look carefully.

The Lord had appeared of old unto me, Saying, yea, I have loved you with an everlasting Love: therefore with loving kindness have I drawn you (Jeremiah 31:3).

<u>Confused Thinking</u>. God is always compassionate. He continually cares for us, even when our will is weak, or thinking confused, and our conscience burdened with guilt. When we are deserted by friends and family and coworkers doesn't seem to understand us, God is there for us. When we have lost the way and lack the courage to go on, we need only listen to hear for God's voice. God's compassion will overcome our shortcomings and our awareness of our sins.

I will heal their backsliding, I will love them freely: for mine anger is turned away from Him (Hosea 14:4).

13. SACRIFICIAL LOVE (JOHN 3:16)

<u>Believe and Trust that Jesus is God</u>. Believing that Jesus is God is more than just an intellectual acceptance. It requires us to put our trust and confidence in Him and accept that He alone can save us. We put Christ in charge of our plans and eternal destiny. We trust

that His words are reliable and that through Him we are given the power to change. Let His promise of everlasting life be yours by simply believing.

For God so loved the world, that He gave His only begotten Son, that whosoever believes in Him should not perish, but have everlasting life (John 3: 16).

Enduring to the End (John 13:1). Jesus knew He would be betrayed by one of His disciples, disowned by another, and deserted by all of them for a time. Still *He showed them the full extent of His love.* God knows us completely, as Jesus knew His disciples (John 2:24-25; and 6:64). He knows the sins we have committed. Still, He loves us. How do you respond to that kind of love?

Now before the feast of the Passover, when Jesus knew that His hour was come that He should depart out of this world unto the Father, having loved His own which were in the world, He loved them unto the end (John 13:1).

Jesus Knew His Disciples. John tells us what Jesus said to His disciples on the night before His death. These words were all spoken in the evening with only the disciples as His audience. He gave final instructions to prepare them for His death and resurrection, events that would change their lives forever (John 13-17)

But Jesus did not commit Himself unto them, because He knew all men, And needed not that any should testify of man: for He knew what was in man (John 2:24-25).

Some Didn't Believe.
But there are some of you that believe not. For Jesus knew from the beginning who they were that believed not, and who should betray Him (John 6:64).

Ardent Affection. Two distinct Greek words for love appear in the Bible. The word *phileo* means "ardent affection and feeling;" or "a type of impulsive love." The other word *agapao* means "to have esteem" or "high regard." In the memorable conversation between Jesus and Peter, there is a play upon these two words

(John 21:15-17*). Jesus asked,* **Simon, do you love me [esteem me]?** but Peter replied, *You know that I love [have ardent affection for] you.* Then Jesus asked, **Simon, do you love [have ardent affection for] me?** And Peter responded that His love was [agape love] a love that held Jesus in high [esteem] and which was more than a [fleeting feeling].

So when they had dined, Jesus said to Simon Peter, **Simon, son of Jonas, love me more than these?** *He Said unto Him, yea, Lord; you know that I love you. He said unto Him,* **Feed my lambs** (John 21:15).

<u>Peter's Three Responses</u>. Jesus asked Peter three times if Peter loved Him. The first time Jesus said, *Do you truly love* (Greek agape) volitional, (self-sacrificial love) *me more than these?* The second time, Jesus focused on Peter alone and still used the word translated into Greek, (agape). The third time, Jesus used the word translated into Greek, (phileo) signifying affection, affinity, or brotherly love and asked, in effect, *Are you even my friend?* Each time Peter responded with the word translated into Greek as (phileo). Jesus doesn't settle for quick, superficial answers.

Jesus has a way of getting to the heart of the matter. Peter had to face His true feelings and motives when Jesus confronted Him. How would you respond if Jesus asked you, *Do you truly love me? Do you really love Jesus? Are you even His friend?*

The warm word *agape* is the characteristic term of Christianity. This word for love is used several different ways in the Bible. Agape love indicates the nature of the love of God toward His beloved Son.

And I have declared unto them your name, and will declare it: that the love wherewith you have loved me may be in them, and I in them (John 17:2).

14. LOVE TOWARD OTHERS (JOHN 3:16)

Believes in agreement that Jesus is God put their trust and confidence in Him that He alone can save them. Believers are putting Christ in charge of their present plans and eternal destiny.

For God so loved the world that He gave His only begotten Son, that whosoever believe in Him should not perish, but have everlasting life (John 3:16).

While we were still sinners . . . (Romans 5:8). These are amazing words. God sent Jesus Christ to die for us, not because we were good enough, but because He loved us. Whenever you feel uncertain about God's love for you, remember that He loved you even before you turned to Him. If God loved you when you were a rebel, He can surely strengthen you that now you love Him in return.

But God commends His love toward us, in that, while we were yet sinners, Christ died for us (Romans 5:8).

15. RESPONSIBILITIES FOR FOLLOWING CHRIST (JOHN 14:21)

Followers Show Their Love by Obeying. This is for those who are followers of Christ, who believe on the Lord Jesus Christ for eternal salvation. Jesus said that His followers show their love for Him by obeying Him. Love is more than words, it is commitment and conduct. If you love Christ, then prove it by obeying what He says in His Word.

He that has my commandments, and keeps them, he it is that loves me: and he that loves me shall be loved of my Father, and I will love him, and will manifest myself to him (John 14:21).

Agape Love. Agape love conveys God's will to His children about their attitude toward one another. Love for one another was a proof to the world of true discipleship. To love others was not just a new commandment.

Love expresses the essential nature of God. Agape love conveys God's will through Jesus Christ to his people about their attitude toward one another. Love for one another is proof to the world of true discipleship (John 13:34-35).

Jesus says that our Christ-like love will show we are His disciples. Do people see petty bickering, jealousy, and division in your church or do they know you are Jesus' followers by your love for one another?

A new commandment I give unto you, that you love one another; as I have loved you, that you also love one another (John 13:34).

Love Others as Jesus Loved Us. Love is more than simply warm feelings. It is an attitude that reveals itself in action. How can we love others as Jesus loves us?

- by helping when it's not convenient,

- by giving when it hurts,

- by devoting energy to others' welfare other than our own, and

- by absorbing hurts from others without complaining or fighting back.

This kind of loving is hard to do. That is why people notice when you do it and know you are empowered by a super-nat-u-ral source, something that exists outside the known force of nature. The Bible has another beautiful description of love (1-Corinthians 13).

16. PETER TRIED TO PROTECT HIMSELF (JOHN 18:25-27)

Peter told Jesus that he was ready to die for Jesus. But Jesus corrected Peter. Jesus knew Peter would deny that he knew Jesus that very night to protect Himself. It is easy to make promises, but God knows the extent of our commitment.

Think Not of Yourself. The Bible teaches us not to think of ourselves more highly than we ought to. Instead of bragging, demonstrate your commitment as you grow in your knowledge of God's Word and in your faith. Read John 18:25-27.

For I say, through the grace given unto me, to every man that is among you, not to think of himself more highly than he ought to think, but to think soberly, according as God has dealt to every man the measure of faith (Romans 12:3).

17. FRUITS OF THE SPIRIT

<u>The Fruits of the Spirit</u>. The fruits of the Spirit is the spontaneous work of the Holy Spirit in us. The Spirit produces these character traits that are found in the nature of Christ. They are the by-products of Christ's control. We can't obtain them by trying to get them without His help. If we want the fruits of the Spirit to grow in us, we must join our lives to Him. We must know Him, love Him, remember Him, and imitate Him. As a result, we will fulfill the intended purpose of the law to love God and our neighbors. Which of these qualities do you want the Spirit to produce in you?

But the fruit of the Spirit is love, joy, peace, longsuffering, gentleness, goodness, faith (Galatians 5:22).

<u>Harmony in God's Law</u>. Because God sent the law and also sent the Spirit, the by-products of the Spirit-filled life are in perfect harmony with the intent of God's law. A person who exhibits the fruit of the Spirit fulfills the law far better than a person who observes the rituals but has little love in their heart. Read Galatians 5:23, *Meekness, temperance: against such there is no law.*

18. LOVE IS LIKE OIL TO THE WHEELS (PSALM 119:32)

<u>Love is like Oil to the Wheels of Obedience</u>. It enables us to run the way of God's commandments. Without such love we are as nothing (1-Corinthians 13:3).

<u>Duty and Expectations</u>. Let us talk a little about run the way of commandments. The more comfort God gives us the more duty He expects from us. When reading Psalm 119:32 we have His resolution to go on vigorously, to run the way of God's commandments through Christ. Those who are going to heaven

should make haste and be still pressing forward. It concerns us with cheerfulness.

We then run the way of our duty, when we are ready to it, and pleasant in it, and lay aside every weight (Hebrews 12:1-2).

We must have the dependence upon God for grace to do so: I shall then abound in thy works, when you shall enlarge my heart.

I will run the way of thy commandments, when you shall enlarge my heart (Psalm 119:32).

A Cloud of Witnesses (Hebrews 12:1-2).
Wherefore seeing we also are compassed about with so great a cloud of witnesses, let us lay aside every weight, and the sin which does so easily beset us, and let us run with patience the race that is set before us. Looking upon Jesus the author and finisher of our faith; who for the joy that was set before Him endured the cross, despising the shame, and is set down at the right hand of the throne of God (Hebrews 12:1-2).

By the Spirit of God through Jesus Christ enlarges the heart of His people when He gives them wisdom, for that is called largeness of heart when He sheds abroad the love of God in the heart and puts gladness there. The joy of our Lord should be wheels to our obedience. Read 1-Kings 4:29.

19. GOD GIVES WISDOM

And God gave Solomon wisdom and understanding exceeding much, and largeness of heart, even as the sand that is on the sea shore (1-Kings 4:29).

Principle of Devotion. Doing good to others will do nothing for us if it be not well done, namely, from a principle of devotion and charity, love to God, and good-will to men. Note that if we leave charity out of religion, the most costly services will be of no avail to us. If we give away all we have while we withhold the heart from God, it will not profit us. Even suffering of the most grievous kind, if we give our bodies to be burnt, without charity it profit nothing (1-Corinthians 13:3).

<u>To Sum up Charity</u>. To sum up the excellences of charity, it is preferred not only to gifts, but to other graces, to faith and hope.

- Faith fixes on the Divine revelation and assents thereto, relying on the divine redeemer.

- Hope fastens on future happiness, and waits for that, but in heaven, faith will be swallowed up in actual sight, and hope, when we see and enjoy.

But there, love will be made perfect. There we shall perfectly love God. There we shall perfectly love one another. Blessed state! How much surpassing the best below! God is love; where God is to be seen as He is face to face, there charity is in its greatest height and there only will it be perfected.

Charity never fails: but whether there be prophecies, they shall fail; whether there be tongues, they shall cease; whether there be knowledge, it shall vanish away (1-Corinthians 13:8)

<u>God is Love</u>.
And we have known and believed the love that God had to us. God is love; and He that dwell in love dwell in God, and God in Him (1-John 4:8; 4:16).

20. ETERNAL PURPOSE

There is an eternal purpose for the office-bearing of professional gifts. It can be stated no clearer than what the three things the verse says: The minister of God works to bring about a perfect unity among God's people. The minister of God is called

- to bring peace and reconciliation to the church ;

- to lead people into perfect harmony and oneness of spirit; and

- to shepherd people out of cliques, divisiveness, murmuring, grumbling, griping, and against a perfect unity.

Now I beseech you, brethren, by the name of our Lord Jesus Christ, that you all speak the same thing, and that there be no divisions among you;

but that you be perfectly joined together in the same mind and in the same judgment (1-Corinthians 1:10).

From whom the whole body fitly joined together, and compacted by that which every joint supping according to the effectual working in the measure of every part, making increase of the body unto the edifying of itself in love (Ephesians 4:16).

UNIT I: WORKSHEET 1

<u>True / False</u>

1. Ephesians chapter _____ verse _____ says: T / F
    The body make increase of the edifying of itself in love.

2. Ephesians chapter 4 verse _____ : *The*   T / F
    whole body fitly joined together and compacted by that which every joint supp according to the effectual working in the measure of every part.

3. "Being a believer" means that we are to put our   T / F
    trust in Jesus.

4. "Being a believer" means that we should put   T / F
    Christ in charge of our present plans and eternal destiny.

5. Because of God's love, would you say it was   T / F
    unconditional which gave Him reason to send His Son into the world to die for the unsaved?

6. Why did God send his Son into the world? Was   T / F
    it because He loved the world that much?

7. John 3: 16 says, *Whosoever believe in him should*   T / F
    not perish . . .

8. John 3:16 says, God loved the world but   T / F
    wouldn't send a son to save it.

UNIT I: WORKSHEET 2

<u>True/False</u>

1. It is recorded that the greatest book of love in the world is the Bible.   T / F

2. It is certainly the most remarkable book of love in the world.   T / F

3. a. It is the greatest love story ever written of God's unconditional love.   T / F
   b. Book_____ Chapter _____
   Verse _____

4. What did Jesus mean by "living water?" in the Old Testament, many verses speak of thirsting after God as one thirsts for water. Is this saying in the Old Testament or is it in the New Testament.   _____

5. Where in the Bible is this: *As the deer thirsts after the water brooks, so thirsts my soul after thee, 0 God.* Psalm 42:3_____ or Psalm 42:1_____

6. Where in the Bible is this: *Jesus answered and said unto her, if you know the gift of God, and who it is that said to you, give me to drink,*
   Book _____ Chapter_____
   Verse_____

7. a. *Jesus said, If you knew who have ask to give to drink, you would have asked of him, and he would have given you living water.* This person a believer.   T / F
   b.   Book   _____
   Chapter_____ Verse_____

8. l-John 4:8 says: "God is love"   T / F

9. Love is not only one of God's attributes; it is also an essential part of his nature. "God is love" the Bible declares his love.
   Book_____ Chapter_____
   Verse_____

10.   The personification of perfect love. Such love surpasses our power of understanding. God's love is total, it reaches every comer of our experience. It is wide. It covers the breadth of our own experience, and it reaches out to the whole world. where in the Bible does it show that Jesus was sent into the world?
Book _____ Chapter_____
Verse_____

11.   a. In the conversation Jesus had with Peter   T / F
concerning his love toward him was a play upon these two words. Jesus asked Peter did he love him. Peter said. "Yes." Jesus asked again, "Peter do you love me." Peter responded that his love for Jesus was [agape love] a love that held Jesus in high esteem and which was more than a fleeting feeling.
b. John 21: Chapter_____ Verse_____

CHAPTER 1: WORKSHEET 3

True/False

1. a. Agape love, the warmest which is the characteristic term of Christianity. This word for love is used several different ways in the Bible. Agape love indicates the nature of the love God has toward His beloved son, and His Son had for Him. Jesus said, *I have declared unto them your name, and will declare it: that the love wherewith you have loved me may be in them, and I in them.*   T / F

2. Jesus said, *I have declared unto them your name, and will declare it: that the love wherewith you have loved me may be in them, and I in them.*
It is found in John 17:26   T / F

3. All this time that Jesus went in and out among them, he made it his business to declare his Father's name to them, and to beget in them a veneration for it. The tendency of all his sermons and to spread the knowledge of him. This is what is being made known by John unto the readers of the world, in saying, *No man has seen God at any time; the only begotten Son, which is in the bosom of the Father, he has declared him.*   T / F

4. *No man has seen God at any time; the only begotten Son, which is in the bosom of the Father, he has declared him.* It is found in John 1:18.   T / F

5. a. What he intended to do yet further for them: I will declare it. To the disciples he planned to give further instruction after his resurrection, and bring them into a much more intimate acquaintance with divine things by the pouring out of the Spirit after his ascension; and to all believers, into whose hearts he had shined, he shines more and more.
b. The Book of John, chapter _____
verse _____   T / F

6. While we were yet sinners, God sent Jesus   T / F
Christ to die for us, not because we were good
enough, but because he didn't care much about
our way of living.

7. When we feel uncertain about God's love for   T / F
us, we can just forget it in knowing that he
doesn't care.

8. He loved us even before we turn to him for   T / F
forgiveness

9. Romans 5:8 says *God commends His love*   T / F
toward us.

10. Romans 5:8 says: But God commends His
love toward us, in that while we were yet
_____, Christ died for us.

CHAPTER 1: WORKSHEET 4

<u>True/False</u>

1. Jesus said that his followers show their love for him by obeying him. Love is more than lovely words; it is commitment and conduct. If you love Christ, then prove it by obeying what he says in his Word. *He that has my commandments, and keeps them, he it is that loves me: and he that loves me shall be loved of my Father, and I will love him, and will manifest myself to him.* This scripture verse is found in John 14:21   T / F

2. Sometimes people wish to know the future so they can prepare for it. God has chosen not to give us this knowledge. He alone knows what will happen.   T / F

3. God tells us all we need to know to prepare for the future.   T / F

4. When we live by his standards, he will not leave us.   T / F

5. He will come to us, He will be in us, and He will show himself to us. God knows what will happen and, because He will be with us through it all, we need not fear.   T / F

6. We don't have to know the future to have faith in God.   T / F

7. We have to have faith in God to be secure about the future.   T / F

8. Agape love conveys God's will to his children about their attitude toward one another. Jesus says that our Christ-like love will show we are his disciples. Do people see petty bickering, jealousy, and division in your church? Or do they know you are Jesus' followers by your love for one another? Can people tell whether you are a follower of Christ with your attitude.   Yes No

9.   John 13:34 says: *New commandment! give unto*   T / F
you, that you love one another, as I have loved
you, that you also love one another.

10   Peter proudly told Jesus that he was ready   T / F
to die for him. But Jesus knew Peter would
deny knowing Jesus that very night to
protect himself. Look at this, *Simon Peter*
stood and warmed himself. They said therefore
unto him, Art not you also one of his disciples?
(Peter denied it) and said, I am not.

11.   *One of the servants of the high priest said, did*   T / F
not I see you in the garden with him? Peter then
denied again, and immediately the cock crowed.

12.   You can lie and get away with it like   T / F
Peter did.

CHAPTER 1: WORKSHEET 5

True/False

1. John says, "God is love," not love is God." T / F

2. Our world, with its shallow and selfish view of love, has turned these words around and contaminated our understanding of love. T / F

3. There is such a thing as stiff love which is hard love. T / F

4. The world thinks that love is what makes a person feel good. T / F

5. It is all right to sacrifice moral principles and others' rights in order to obtain such "love." T / F

6. But that isn't real love; it is the exact opposite which is selfishness. T / F

7. Real love is like God, who is holy, just, and perfect. T / F

8. If we truly know God, we will love as he does. T / F

9. a. The scriptures says: *He that loves not, knows not God; for God is love.* T / F
   b. Book _____ Chapter_____ Verse_____

10. As the Spirit of truth is known by doctrine this spirits are to be tried, it is known by love likewise; and so here follows a strong fervent exhortation to holy Christian love: *Beloved, let us love one another*
    I-John 4:7_____ or 2-John 3:8 _____

11. *Beloved, let us love one another: for love is of God.* T / F

12. The Spirit of God is the Spirit of love. The new nature in the children of God is the offspring of his love. T / F

13. The fruit of the Spirit is love. T / F

14. a. The 7 fruits of the Spirit are: love, joy, peace, longsuffering, gentleness, goodness, and faith. T / F
    b. Book _____ Chapter_____ Verse_____

CHAPTER 1: WORKSHEET 6

1. Love found its perfect expression in the Lord Jesus Christ. Christian love is the fruit of the spirit of Jesus in the believer. It is the spontaneous work of the Holy Spirit in us. The Spirit produces these character traits that are found in the nature of Christ.　　T / F

2. The Holy Spirit is the by-products of Christ's control.　　T / F

3. We can't obtain them by trying to get them without his help.　　T / F

4. If we want the fruit of the Spirit to grow in us, we must join our lives to His. The Scripture in John says: *If we abide in Him, and He in you. As the branch cannot bear fruit of itself, except it abide in the vine; no more can you, except you abide in me.*　　T / F

5. *I am the vine, you are the branches. Hhe that abide in me., and I in him, the same bring forth much fruit: for without me you can do nothing.* b. This is found in John 15:4-5.　　T / F

6. *We must know him, love him, remember him* is found in 1-Corinthians 11:23-34.　　T / F

7. a. Lord's Supper, is in the Old Testament. b. Book _____ Chapter_____ Verse_____　　T / F

8. We also must imitate him. As a result, we will· fulfill the intended purpose of the law to love God and our neighbors.　　T / F

9.   Which of these qualities do you want the   All
     Spirit to produce in you?   None

10   Do you need any of this to work in you?   Yes
                                                       No

11. Because the God who sent the law also sent   T / F
     the Spirit.

12. The by-products of the Spirit-filled life are in T / F
     perfect harmony with the intent. of God's law.

13. A person who exhibits the fruit of the Spirit   T / F
     fulfills the law.

14. Far better than a person who observes the   T / F
     rituals but has little love in their heart.

CHAPTER 1: WORKSHEET 7

True/False

1. a. According to the Psalm, the more comfort   T / F
    God gives us the more duty he expects from
    us, his resolution to go on vigorously in
    religion.
    b. Book _____ Chapter_____
    Verse_____

2. The teachings of the Psalm is that *I will run*   T / F
    the way of your commandments, when you shall
    enlarge my heart. This is in Psalms 119:32.

3. Those who are looking to go to heaven should   T / F
    make haste thither and be still pressing
    forward.

4. a. It is our concern to redeem the time and   T / F
    take pains, and to go on in our business with
    cheerfulness. b. Book _____
    Chapter_____ Verse_____

5. We then run the way of our duty, when we   T / F
    are ready to it, and pleasant in it, and lay aside
    every weight

6. a. *Redeem the time because the days are evil.*   T / F
    b. Book _____ Chapter_____
    Verse_____

7. It is a person's dependence upon the Lord for   T / F
    grace to run the way of the believer for God's
    service.

8. The Psalms say when you shall enlarge my   T / F
    heart, *Is it God's Spirit, that enlarges the heart of*
    his people when He gives them wisdom for that He
    called largeness of heart.

9. Psalm 119:32 says, *I will run the way of your*   T / F
    commandment, when you shall enlarge my heart.

10   When he sheds abroad the love of God in the   T / F
        heart, and puts gladness there. The joy of
        our Lord should be wheels to our obedience.
        This love is like oil to our wheels of obedience
        to the Word of God through our Lord Jesus
        Christ. It enables us to run the way of God's
        commandments.

11.   Ephesians 5:14 says that since exposing sin   T / F
        is beneficial, God invites the unbeliever in
        saying *you that sleep are to turn from sin (arise*
        from the dead) with the promise that he will be
        granted the spiritual enlightenment and help
        needed Christ shall give you light.

12.   Ephesians 5:15 says to *walk circumspectly not as*   T / F
        fools, but as wise.

CHAPTER 2.
MAN'S RELATIONSHIP
WITH GOD

1. PHYSICAL LIFE (GENESIS 2:7)

<u>Breath of Life</u>. For people, animals and plants the physical life is the time between birth and death. Because God is the source of life it is a gift from Him. He first filled Adam with the breath of life and He continues to be the source of all life.

And the Lord God formed man of the dust of the ground, and breathed into his nostrils the breath of life; and man became a living soul (Genesis 2:7).

<u>Dust of the Ground</u>. "From the dust of the ground" implies that there is nothing fancy about the elements making up our bodies. The body is a lifeless shell until God brings it alive with His "breath, if life." When God removes His life-giving breath, our bodies once again return to dust. Our life and worth come from God's Spirit.

<u>The God of Creation</u>. Many people boast of their achievements and abilities as though they were the originator of their abilities. In reality, our worth comes not from our achievements but from the God of the universe or should I say the God of creation of everything that moves upon the earth. It is God who chooses to give us the mysterious and miraculous life. We must value life just as God does.

<u>Expanding the New Testament</u>. The New Testament expanded on the Old Testament idea of life. The word life began to refer to more than physical existence. It took on a strong spiritual meaning, after referencing to the spiritual life result from <u>man's relationship with God</u>.

2. RELATIONSHIP WITH GOD (JOHN 17:3)

Eternal Life and Fellowship with God. Eternal life means more than eternal existence. Eternal life refers to eternal fellowship with God.

This is life eternal, Jesus declared, *that they may know you, the only true God, and Jesus Christ whom you have sent.*

And this is life eternal that they might know You the only true God, and Jesus Christ, whom You have sent (John 17:3).

How Can We Get Eternal Life? Answer: Jesus tells us clearly that by knowing God the Father himself through His Son, Jesus Christ. Eternal life requires entering into a personal relationship with God in Jesus Christ or rather in God through Jesus Christ. When we admit to our sin and turn away from it, Christ's love will live in us by the Holy Spirit.

A Positive Relationship with God. Eternal life is the highest quality of life. According to the apostle Paul, it is freedom from sin, holiness, and a positive relationship with God through our Lord Jesus Christ. This is in contrast to spiritual death which results from a life of sin.

What fruit had you then those things whereof you are ashamed? For the end of those things is death. But now being made free from sin, and become Servants to God, you have your fruit unto holiness, and the end everlasting life for the wages of sin is death; but the gift of God is eternal life through Jesus Christ our Lord (Romans 6:21-23).

Every Person Must Choose. It is impossible to be neutral. Every person has a master. It is either God or sin. A Christian is not someone who cannot sin, but someone who is no longer a slave to sin. They belong to God. Eternal life comes through faith in Jesus Christ who taught us, *He who believes in me has everlasting life.*

3. ETERNAL LIFE THROUGH FAITH

The Symbolic Meaning of Life. This symbolic meaning of life appears frequently in the gospel of John. Of Jesus, John wrote, *in Him was life and the life was the light of men.*

Verily, verily, I say unto you, He that believes on me has everlasting life (John 6:47).

Believes as used here means "continues to believe." We do not believe merely once; we continue to believe in and trust Jesus.

Spiritual Bread. The religious leaders frequently asked Jesus to prove to them why we was better than the prophets they already had. Jesus referred to the manna that Moses had given their ancestors in the desert. That bread was physical and temporal. But they had to get more bread every day, and that bread could not keep them from dying. Jesus, who is much greater than Moses, offers himself as the spiritual bread from heaven that satisfies completely and leads to eternal life.

In Him is Life. When God created, He made something from nothing. Because we are created beings, we have no basis for pride. Remember that we exist only because God made us, and we have special gifts only because God gave them to us. To God we are something valuable and unique; apart from God we are nothing, and if we try to live without Him, we will be abandoning the purpose for which we were made.

In Him was life; and the life was the light of man (John 1:4).

4. REGENERATION (MATTHEW 19:28)

Changed through Regeneration. Regeneration is the change brought about in a person's life by an act of God. In regeneration a person's sinful nature is changed, and he is able to respond to God in faith. The word regeneration occurs only in the New Testament, but the concept or idea is common throughout the Bible.

The Darkness Has Not Understood. *The darkness has not understood.* It means the darkness of evil never has and never will overcome or extinguish God's light. The Creator of life is Jesus and His life brings light to mankind. In His light we see ourselves as we really are as sinners who need a Savior. We can avoid walking blindly and falling into sin when we follow Jesus, the true Light. He lights the path ahead of us so we can see how to live.

Ask yourself, have you allowed the light of Christ to shine into your life? If not, let Christ guide your life, and you will never need to stumble in darkness. Being born again helps you to understand that you will never again walk in darkness.

And Jesus said unto them, Verily I say unto you, that you who have followed me, in the regeneration when the Son of man shall sit in the throne of His glory, you also shall sit upon twelve thrones, judging the twelve Tribes of Israel (Matthew 19:28).

Difficulty of Salvation for the Rich. Christ had a discussion with His disciples during their meal with the rich man.

Christ took the occasion from thence to show the difficulty of the salvation of the rich people in (Matthew 19:23-29).

5. THE WORK OF SALVATION (TITUS 3:4-6)

Redemptive Work of the Trinity. All three persons of the Trinity are mentioned in Titus 3:4-6 because all three participate in the work of salvation. Based upon the redemptive work of His Son, the Father forgives and sends the Holy Spirit to wash away our sins and continually renew us.

But after that the kindness and the love of God our Savior toward man appeared, not by works of righteousness which we have done, but according to His mercy. He saved us, by the washing of regeneration, and renewing of the Holy Ghost, which He shed on us abundantly through Jesus Christ our Savior (Titus 3:4-6).

6. REGENERATION MEANS "BORN AGAIN" (JOHN 3:1-12)

<u>Concept of Regeneration</u>. As it was said regeneration only occurs in the New Testament but the concept or idea is common throughout the Bible. The meaning of regeneration is "born again." There is a first birth and a second birth. The first, as Jesus said to Nicodemus.

Verily, verily, I say unto you, Except a man be born again, He cannot see the kingdom of God (John 3:3).

<u>Pharisees of the Sanhedrin</u>. Nicodemus was a Pharisee and a member of the ruling council called the Sanhedrin. The Pharisees were a group of religious leaders who Jesus and John the Baptist often criticized for being hypocrites as expressed in the notes in Matthew 3:7.

But when He saw many of the Pharisees and Sadducees come to His baptism, He said unto them O generation of vipers, who has warned you to flee from the wrath to come? (Matthew 3:7).

Every biblical command to man is to undergo a radical change of character from self-centeredness to God-centeredness is. It is in effect an appeal to be "born again."

7. THE NEED FOR SALVATION

<u>Encountering Strife and Difficulty in Our Lives</u>. The need for salvation goes back to man's removal from the Garden of Eden after the fall. It has been said many times before that man's life was marked by strife and difficulty. Once man takes His eyes off of God's purposes for him, the highlights of life take place in his life. Then man comes to a point of life where he feels sorry for himself and becomes angry with himself and God.

<u>Jeremiah Was Angry and Afraid</u>. Similarly Jeremiah had taken his eyes off God's purpose and was feeling sorry for himself. Jeremiah was angry, hurt, and afraid. However, in response, God did not get angry at Jeremiah. God answered by rearranging Jeremiah's

priorities. As God's mouthpiece, Jeremiah was to influence the people, not let them influence him. There are three important lessons in this passage.

(1)   In prayer we can reveal our deepest thoughts to God.

(2)   God expects us to trust him, no matter what.

(3)   We are here to influence others for God.

And I will make you unto this people a fenced brazen wall: and they shall fight against you, but they shall not prevail against you: For I am with you to save you and to deliver you, said the Lord (Jeremiah 15:20)

8. THE EARTH WAS CORRUPT (GENESIS 6:11-13)

Corruption and Violence Dominated the World. Increasingly man's life became marked by strife and difficulty with corruption and violence dominating the world. It was corrupt before God. Man worshiped images; they were corrupt and wicked. God was despised and held in contempt and man defied Him. The earth was filled with violence and injustice towards each other. There was no order, no government. No one was safe in the possession of that which he had the most clear and incontestable right to, not even the most innocent life. There was nothing but murder and rape.

The Shame of Human Nature. This wickedness was the shame of human nature, and continues to be the ruin of human society. Therefore, when you talk about the need for salvation and entering into the kingdom of heaven with all of this going on, you must be born again. No one can enter into the kingdom of God with a wicked and corrupt nature. This is the need for salvation.

The earth also was corrupt before God, and the earth was filled with violence. And God looked upon the earth, and, behold, it was corrupt; for all flesh had corrupted his way upon the earth (Genesis 6:11-13).

Without Conscience and Fear of God. Take away conscience and the fear of God and men will become like beasts and devils to one another, like the fishes of the sea, where the greater devour the less. When sin fills the earth with violence, it turns the world into a wilderness, into a cock-pit.

The proof and evidence of it were undeniable; for God looked upon the earth, and was an eye-witness to the corruption that was in it, of which it was before when He saw that the wickedness of man was great in the earth, and that every imagination of the thoughts of His heart was only evil continually (Genesis 6:5).

All of this will help us to understand when the need for salvation first started. We need the salvation of God today, although salvation in the Old Testament is different from the New Testament salvation.

9. DELIVERENCE AND SALVATION

<u>Deliverance From the Power of Sin (Redemption)</u>. In the Old Testament, the word salvation sometimes refers to deliverance from danger, deliverance of the weak from an oppressor, or the healing of sickness, and deliverance from blood guilt and its consequences. It may also refer to national deliverance from military threat or release from captivity. But salvation finds its deepest meaning in the spiritual realm of life. Man's universal need for salvation is one of the clearest teachings of the Bible.

<u>Noah was God's First Act of Salvation</u>. God performed the first act of salvation by saving Noah and His family. It was the basis of another chance for mankind. Noah's family was viewed by the apostle Peter as a pattern of that full salvation which we receive in Christ. Salvation in Christ Jesus is the eternal salvation when He comes back for His church.

Here are additional scriptures about salvation in the Old Testament which you can read: Jeremiah 15:20; Psalm 35:9-10; Isaiah 38:20; Exodus 14:13; and Psalm 14:7.

10. OLD TESTAMENT SALVATION

Exodus: The Old Testament Experience of Salvation. The central Old Testament experience of salvation is the Exodus (Exodus 12:40; 14:31). Much of Israel's worship of God was a renewal of this mighty experience that brought them from tyranny in Egypt to freedom in the promised land (Exodus 13:3-16). The mighty saving power of God was demonstrated dramatically as the Israelites formed a holy nation of priestly servants of the Lord (Exodus 19:4-6). The Exodus became a pattern of salvation through which God's future deeds of redemption would be understood.

Babylon Captivity Created an Expectation of a New and Better Exodus. Just as the Exodus symbolized their salvation, the captivity of the Israelites in Babylon was a disastrous return to bondage. The people responded to this plight with expectation of a new and better Exodus (Isaiah 43:14-16) in which God would forgive their sins and restore their hearts to faithfulness (Jeremiah 31:31-34). This hope for a new Exodus encompassed an expectation of a full realization of the rule of God (Ezekiel 36:22-38).

The Day of the Lord. Since God was Lord and had shown Himself to be righteous and faithful He must also one day overpower His enemies and perfect the life of His people. This hope was expressed through the concept of the "day of the Lord" as described by the Old Testament prophets (Joel 2:1-11; Amos 9:11-15) but this also focused on the role of the Anointed king and the coming of the Messiah (Psalm 2). Even Israel's return from the captivity failed to fulfill all their hope (Haggai 2:3), so a new understanding arose. The full realization of God's purpose of salvation would involve the completely new age (Isaiah 65: 17-25). This doctrine of salvation reached its fulfillment in the death of Christ Jesus on our behalf.

11. DOCTRINE OF SALVATION

Doctrine of Salvation Fulfilled by Christ. Jesus' mission was to save the world from sin and the wrath of God (Matthew 1:21; John 12:47; Roman 5:9). During His earthly ministry, salvation was brought to us by His presence and the power of faith (Luke 19:9-10).

Now our salvation is based on Christ's death and resurrection (Mark 10:25).

Paul's Message of Salvation. The salvation that comes through Christ may be described in three tenses: (past) (present) and (future). When a person believes in Christ He is saved (Acts 16:31). Read some of Paul's writings concerning being saved. Paul did not leave His message unfinished. He confronted His listeners with Jesus' resurrection and its meaning to all people either blessing or punishment. The Greeks had no concept of judgment. Most of them preferred worshiping many gods instead of just one, and the concept of resurrection was unbelievable and offensive to them. Paul did not hold back the truth, no matter what they might think of it. Paul often changed his approach to fit his audience, but he never changed his basic message.

The time of this ignorance God winked at; but now command all men everywhere to repent. Because He has appointed a day, in the which He will judge the world in righteousness by that man whom He has ordained; whereof He had given assurance unto all men, in that He had raised Him from the dead (Acts 17:30-31).

Ignore Temptation. When you regard sin's appeal as dead and lifeless, you can ignore temptation when it comes.

Paul said, *If you live after the flesh, you shall die: but if you through the Spirit do mortify the deeds of the body, you shall live* (Romans 8:13).

But we are also in the process of being saved from the power of sin. In light of "working out your own salvation" was the preceding exhortation to unity, which means the entire church was to work together to rid themselves of divisions and discord (Philippians 2:12).

12. THE POWER OF CHRIST

The Power of Christ's Resurrection. God has released into our lives today the power of Christ's resurrection (Roman 6:4) and allows us a foretaste of our future life as His children (2-Corinthians 1:22; Ephesians 1: 14). Our experience of salvation will be complete when Christ returns (Hebrews 9:28) and the kingdom of God is fully revealed (Matthew 13:41-43).

Redemption: Deliverance by Payment of a Price. In the New Testament redemption refers to salvation from sin, death, and the wrath of God by Christ's sacrifice. In the Old Testament the word redemption refers to

- Redemption by a kinsman (Leviticus 25:24-25; Ruth 4:6; Jeremiah 32:7-8),

- Rescue or deliverance (Numbers 3:49); and

- Ransom (Psalm 111:9; 130:7).

In the New Testament it refers to loosing (Luke 2:38; Hebrews 9:12) and looking away (Luke 21:28; Romans 3:24; Ephesians 1:14). In the Old Testament redemption was applied to property, animals, persons, and the nation of Israel as a whole. In nearly every instance freedom from obligation, bondage, or danger was secured by the payment of a price, a ransom, bribe, satisfaction, or sum of money paid to obtain freedom, favor, or reconciliation. Men redeemed property, animals, and individuals (slaves, prisoners, indentured relatives) who are legally obligated to God or in bondage for other reasons. God alone is able to redeem from

- the slavery of sin (Psalm 130:7-8),

- enemy oppressors (Deuteronomy 15:15), and

- the power of death (Job 19:25-26; Psalm 49:8-9).

CHAPTER 2: WORKSHEET 1

1. Since God was Lord and had shown Himself to be righteous and faithful, He must one day overpower His enemies and perfect the life of His people. This hope is expressed through the concept of the "day of the Lord" as described by the Old Testament prophet in Joel 2:1-11.   T / F

2. Joel 2:11 says, *The Lord shall utter his voice before his [followers/army].*   T / F

3. Joel 2:5 says, *Like the noise of [thunder/chariots] on the top of mountains shall they leap, like the noise of a flame of fire that devoureth the stubble, as a strong people set in battle array.*   T / F

4. Joel 2 verse _____ says, *A fire devoureth before them, and behind them a flame burned: the land is as the Garden of Eden before them, and behind them a desolate [wilderness/desert], and nothing shall escape them.*

5. Amos 9:9 says, *All the sinners of my people shall die by the sword,* which means the evil shall not overtake nor prevent us.   T / F

6. Amos 9: verse _____ says, *In that day will I raise up the tabernacle of [David/Moses] that is fallen, and close up the breaches thereof: and I will build it as in the day of old.*

CHAPTER 2: WORKSHEET 2

True/False

1. Jeremiah 31:31 says, *Behold, the days come said the Lord, that I will make a new covenant with the house of Israel, and with the house of Judah.*   T / F

2. Just as the Exodus symbolized their salvation, the captivity of the Israelites in Babylon was a disastrous return to bondage. The people responded to this plight with expectations of a new and better Exodus. Isaiah 43:14-16 tells the story of the Exodus.   T / F

3. The mighty saving power of God was demonstrated dramatically as the Israelites formed as a holy nation of priestly servants of the Lord. In Exodus 19:4 the Lord said this unto them, *You have seen what I did unto the Egyptians.*   T / F

4. *You shall be unto me a kingdom of priests.* This is Exodus 19:6.   T / F

5. *If you will obey my voice indeed, and keep my covenant, then you shall be a peculiar treasure unto me above all people: for all the earth is mine.* This is Exodus 19:7.   T / F

6. Much of Israel's worship of God was a renewal of this mighty experience that brought them from tyranny in Egypt to freedom in the Promised Land. Exodus 13:3-16 gives the central Old Testament experience of salvation of the Israelites.   T / F

7.   Exodus 13:3-16 [verse_____]And Moses said   T / F
*and it shall be when the Lord brings you into the
land of the _____*
*[verse _____] No leavened bread shall be_____
with you.*
*[verse _____] _____days you shall
eat unleavened bread [verse _____] and you shall
show your son in that day, saying, this is done
because of that which the Lord did unto me when I
came forth out of _____.*
[verse_____] It shall be for a _____.

CHAPTER 2: WORKSHEET 3
OLD TESTAMENT EXPERIENCE OF SALVATION (EXODUS 12:40)

<u>True/False</u>

1. The central Old Testament experience of salvation is the Exodus were those who dwelt in Egypt. These are the people who are called the children of Israel in Exodus 12:40. T / F

2. These children, dwelled in Egypt for four hundred and thirty years. T / F

3. a. The same day it came to pass, that all the hosts of the Lord went out from the land of Egypt?
b. Found in which verse 41 [] or 42 [] T / F

4. Exodus 12:39 says, *Because they were thrust out of Egypt and could not tarry, neither had they prepared for themselves any victual.* T / F

5. Exodus 14:31 says, *And Israel saw that great work which the Lord did upon the [Egyptians/Ismalites]: and the people feared the Lord, believed the Lord, and his servant Moses.* T / F

6. Exodus 14:31: This is a part of the [covenant/salvation] they saw or received of the Lord their God. T / F

EXPULSION FROM THE GARDEN OF EDEN

7. The need for [salvation/forgiveness] goes back to man's removal from the Garden of Eden. T / F

8.　　Since the Garden of Eden man's life was　T / F
　　　marked with strife, difficulty, and it was
　　　increasingly corrupt and violent.

9.　　The Scriptural reference that gives the
　　　removal of man from the Garden of Eden.
　　　Book _____ Chapter_____
　　　Verse_____

CHAPTER 2: WORKSHEET 4
WICKEDNESS OF MANKIND (GENESIS 6:11-13)

<u>True/False</u>

1. God said unto Noah, *the end of all flesh is come before me.*
   This Genesis 6 verse 11 [] or verse 13 []

2. *The earth also was corrupt before God, and the earth was filled with violence.* This is Genesis 6 verse 2 [] verse 3 [] or verse 11 []

3. *God looked upon the earth and behold, it was corrupt; for all flesh had corrupted his way upon the earth.* Genesis 6 verse _____.

4. Deliverance from the power of sin. In the Old Testament, the word salvation sometimes refers to deliverance from danger. Jeremiah 15: 20 says, *And I will make you unto this people a fenced [stone/] brazen wall: and they shall fight against you, but they shall not prevail against you: for I am with you to save you and to deliver you, said the Lord.* T / F

5. Salvation is in the power of God. T / F

6. Psalm 51:14 says, *Deliver me from blood guiltiness, 0 God, you God of my Salvation: and my tongue shall sing aloud of your righteousness.* T / F

7. a. Salvation finds its deepest meaning in the Spiritual realm of life. T / F
   b. Book _____ Chapter_____ Verse_____

8. a. Man's universal need for salvation is one of the clearest teachings of the Bible. T / F
   b. Book _____ Chapter_____ Verse_____

9. The death of Christ was the fulfillment of salvation for mankind today. Yes No

46

10   Jesus' mission was to save the world from sin   T / F
      and the wrath of God.

11. Matthew 1:21 says, *You shall call his name Jesus:*   T / F
      for he shall save his people from their sins.

12. John 12:47 says, *If any man hear my words, and*   T / F
      believe not, I judge him not.

13. Romans 5:9 says, *Much more then being now*   T / F
      justified by his blood, we shall be saved from wrath
      through him.

CHAPTER 3. THE LIFE OF JESUS CHRIST

1. AGAPE LOVE

Love expresses the essential nature of God. Agape love conveys God's will through Jesus Christ to his people about their attitude toward one another. Love for one another is proof to the world of true discipleship (John 13:34-35).

2. BIRTH AND UPBRINGING OF JESUS

Significance of the Messiah. The twofold designation of Jesus Christ combines the personal name of Jesus and the title Christ, which means the "anointed" or "Messiah." The significance of this title became clear during the scope of His life and ministry.

Jesus was born in Bethlehem, a town about ten kilometers (six miles) south of Jerusalem, toward the end of Herod the Great's reign as king of the Jews in or around (37-4 B.C.). Early in Jesus' life He was taken to Nazareth, a town of Galilee. There He was brought up by His mother, Mary, and His father, Joseph. It is believed that He was brought up as a carpenter by trade as was Joseph His father. At this time He was known as "Jesus of Nazareth" or more fully, as "Jesus of Nazareth, the son of Joseph."

3. THE CALL OF PHILIP (JOHN 1:45)

The Call of Philip and Nathanael. Philip was called immediately by Christ Himself, not like Andrew who was directed to Christ by John (aka Peter) who was invited by his brother. God has various methods of bringing His chosen ones home to Himself. But whatever means He uses, He is not tied to any. Philip was called in a preventing way: Jesus found Philip.

Philip find Nathanael, and said unto him, we have found him, of whom Moses in the law, and the prophets, did write, Jesus of Nazareth, the son of Joseph (John 1:45).

Christ sought us and found us, before we made any enquiries after Him. The name Philip is of Greek origin, and much used among the Gentiles, which some make an instance of the degeneracy of the Jewish church at this time, and their conformity to the nation; yet Christ changed His name.

4. JESUS WAS FIRSTBORN

Jesus was a First-born Child. He had four brothers (James, Joses, Judas and Simon) and an unspecified number of sisters. Joseph apparently died before Jesus began His public ministry. Mary and the rest of the family became members of the church of Jerusalem after Jesus' death and resurrection.

Rejected by His Peers. Before Jesus' death He was teaching effectively and wisely but the people of His hometown saw Him as only a carpenter. "'He's no better than we are; he's just a common laborer," they said. They were offended that others could be impressed by Jesus and follow him. They rejected His authority because He was one of their peers. They thought they knew him but their preconceived notions about who He was made it impossible for them to accept His message. Don't let prejudice blind you to the truth. As you learn more about Jesus, try to see Him for who He really is.

Is not this the carpenter, the son of Mary, the brother of James, and Joses, and of Juda, and Simon? And are not His sisters here with us? And they were offended at Him (Mark 6:3).

5. LEARNING WHO JESUS IS (LUKE 2:41-52)

The Firstborn of Egypt and Passover. Passover commemorated the Jew's escape from Egypt when God had killed the Egyptian firstborn but had passed over Israelite homes. Passover was the most important of the three annual festivals.

According to God's law, every male was required to go to Jerusalem three times a year for the great festivals. It was in the spring when the festival celebrations would take place followed immediately by the week-long feast of unleavened Bread.

Three times in a year shall all your males appear before the Lord your God in the place which He shall choose; in the feast of unleavened bread, and in the feast of weeks, and in the feast of tabernacles: and they shall not appear before the Lord empty: Every man shall give as He is able, according to the blessing of the Lord your God which He has given you (Deuteronomy 16:16-17)

Family Trip to Jerusalem. The only incident preserved from Jesus' first 30 years after His infancy was His trip to Jerusalem with Joseph and Mary when He was 12 years old. Since He was known in Nazareth as "the carpenter" He may have taken Joseph's place as the family bread-winner at an early age. *Now His parents went to Jerusalem every year at the feast of the Passover.* There are other verses related to this in Luke 2:42-52. You will also read in Mark 6:3 concerning the question of Jesus being a carpenter and asking about His brothers and sisters.

6. POLITICAL UNREST IN ISRAEL

The Province of Galilee. Galilee was the province in Israel where Jesus lived and was ruled by Herod Antipas, youngest son of Herod the Great. The area where Jesus lived was not directly involved in a revolt, but the sympathies of many Galileans were probably stirred. No doubt the boys of Nazareth discussed this issue which they heard their elders debating. Jesus referred to this event 24 years later (Mark12:13-17).

Jesus Viewed as a Threat by the Pharisees. The Pharisees did not like Jesus because He exposed their hypocrisy. The Herodians also saw Jesus as a threat. Supporters of the dynasty of Herod the Great had lost political control. As a result of reported unrest Rome deposed Archelaus, Hero's son, with authority over Judea, and replaced Him with a Roman governor (Pontius Pilate). The Herodians feared that Jesus would cause still more political unrest allowing that Roman leaders to step down and be replaced by a descendant of Herod.

<u>Tribute to Caesar</u>

[13] And they sent unto Him certain of the Pharisees and of the Herodians, to catch Him in His words. [14] And when they were come, they said unto him, Master, we know that you art, and care for no man: for you regard not the person of man, but teach the way of God in truth: is it lawful to give tribute to Caesar, or not? [15] Shall we give, or shall we not give? But He, knowing their hypocrisy, said unto them, **Why temp you me? Bring me a penny, that I may see it.** *[16] And they brought it. And He said unto them,* **Whose is this image and superscription?** *And they said unto him, [17] Caesar's and Jesus answering said unto them,* **Render to Caesar the things that are Caesar's and to God the things that are God's** *and they marveled at him* (Mark 12:13-17).

<u>The Anti-Roman Revolt at Sepphoris</u>. Sepphoris was located about six kilometers which is about four miles northwest of Nazareth. Nazareth had been the center of an anti Roman revolt during Jesus' infancy. The village was destroyed by the Romans, but it was soon rebuilt by Herod Antipas. Antipas lived there as tetrarch of Galilee and Perea until he founded a new capital for his principality at Tiberius on the western shore of the Lake of Galilee A.D. 22. Reports of happenings at his court, while he lived in Sepphoris were probably carried to Nazareth.

<u>The Geography of the Land of Israel</u>. Sites of events from Israel's history could be seen from the slopes above Nazareth. To the south stretched the valley of Jezreel where great battles had been fought in earlier days. Beyond the Valley of Jezreel was Mount Gilboa where King Saul fell in battle with the Philistines. To the east Mount Tabor rose to 562 meters (1,843 feet), the highest elevation in that part of the country.

A growing boy would readily find his mind moving back and forth between the stirring events of former days and the realities of the contemporary situation: the all pervasive presence of the Romans.

7. BEGINNINGS OF JESUS' MINISTRY

<u>John the Baptist</u>. Jesus began His public ministry when He sought baptism at the hands of John the Baptist. John preached between A. D. 27 and 28 in the Lower Jordan Valley and baptized those who wished to give expression to their repentance. The descent of the dove as Jesus came up out of the water was a sign that He was the one anointed by the Spirit of God as the servant-Messiah of His people.

<u>The Purpose of Jesus' Baptism</u>. John had been explaining that Jesus' baptism would be much greater than his. When Jesus came to John and asked to be baptized, John felt unqualified. He wanted to be baptized by Jesus. Why did Jesus ask to be baptized? It was not for repentance for sin because Jesus never sinned. Rather, it was "to fulfill all righteousness"--to accomplish God's mission. Jesus saw His baptism as advancing God's work. Jesus was baptized because:

- He was confessing sin on behalf of the nation as Nehemiah, Ezra, Moses, and Daniel had done.

- He was showing support for what John was doing.

- He was inaugurating His public ministry.

- He was identifying with the penitent people of God, not with the critical Pharisees who were only watching.

Jesus, the perfect man, didn't need baptism for sin but He accepted baptism in obedient service to the Father and God showed His approval.

<u>Expression of Repentance</u>. If John baptized for repentance from sin, why was Jesus baptized? While even the greatest prophets Isaiah, Jeremiah, Ezekiel had to confess their sinfulness and their need for repentance, Jesus didn't need to admit sin; He was sinless. It is important to understand this.

- It was the beginning of His mission to bring the message of salvation to all people.

- It was to show support for John's ministry.

- It was to identify with our humanness and sin.

- It was an example for us to follow.

We know John's baptism was different from Christian baptism in the church because Paul had John's followers baptized again.

And it came to pass in those days that Jesus came from Nazareth of Galilee and was baptized of John in Jordan (Mark 1:9).

8. THE HOLY SPIRIT

"Incomplete" Christians. John's baptism was a sign of repentance from sin only, not a sign of new life in Christ. Like Apollos (Acts 18:24-26) the Ephesian believers needed further instruction on the message. They did not understand the significance of Christ's death and resurrection or the work of the Holy Spirit. Becoming a Christian involves turning from sin in repentance and turning to Christ by faith. These "believers" were incomplete.

This is something we Christians should seek to learn more about Jesus and the Holy Spirit's way of working through Christ in the believers by faith. I will give Scriptures concerning this as I go through it so that you will have a better understanding. In the book of Acts, believers received the Holy Spirit in a variety of ways. All of this is concerning the baptism of the Holy Spirit through the baptism of the water which is a symbol of Christ's death, burial, and resurrection.

Receiving the Holy Spirit. Usually the Holy Spirit would fill a person as soon as they profess having faith in Christ. Here that filling happened later because these disciples' knowledge was incomplete. God was confirming to these believers who did not initially know about the Holy Spirit that they were a part of the church. The Holy Spirit's filling endorsed them as believers.

Pentecost Described in the Book of Acts. Pentecost was the formal event in which the outpouring of the Holy Spirit was God's way of uniting new believers to the church. The mark of the true church is not merely the right doctrine but right actions and the true evidence of the Holy Spirit's work.

He said unto them, have you received the Holy Ghost since you believed? And they said unto him, we have not so much as heard whether there be any Holy Ghost [3] And He said unto them, unto what then were you baptized? And they said, unto John's baptism. [4] Then said Paul, John verily baptized with the baptism of repentance, saying unto the people, that they should believe on Him that should come after him, that is, on Christ Jesus. [5] When they heard this, they were baptized in the name of the Lord Jesus Christ (Acts 19:2-5)

Paul's Message of Resurrection. Paul did not leave His message unfinished. He confronted His listeners with Jesus' resurrection and its meaning to all people as either blessing or punishment. The Greeks had no concept of judgment. Most of them preferred worshiping many gods instead of just one, and the concept of resurrection was unbelievable and offensive to them. Paul did not hold back the truth, no matter what they might think of it. Paul often changed his approach to fit his audience, but he never changed his basic message.

And the time of this ignorance God winked at; but now commands all men everywhere to repent (Acts 17:30).

9. LUKE RECORDED THE BAPTISM OF JESUS (LUKE 3:21-22)

Luke Emphasizes Jesus' Human Nature. Jesus was born to humble parents, a birth unannounced except to shepherds and foreigners. His baptism was the first public declaration of Jesus' ministry. Instead of going to Jerusalem and identifying with the established religious leaders, Jesus went to a river and identified himself with those who were repenting of sin. When Jesus visited the temple at age 12 He understood His mission.

Lord, now latest you your servant depart in Peace, according to your word (Luke 2:29).

At His baptism 18 years later, Jesus began carrying out His mission. As Jesus prayed God spoke and confirmed His decision to act. God was breaking into human history through Jesus the Christ.

<u>Significance of Baptism</u>. If baptism was a sign of repentance from sin, why did Jesus ask to be baptized? Several explanations are often given:

- Jesus' baptism was one step in fulfilling His earthly mission of identifying with our humanity and sin.

- By endorsing the rite of baptism, Jesus was giving us an example to follow; He was being baptized for the sins of the nation.

<u>The Holy Spirit and the Trinity</u>. The Holy Spirit's appearance in the form of a dove showed that God's plan for salvation was centered in Jesus. Jesus was the perfect human who didn't need baptism for repentance, but He was baptized on our behalf. This is one of several places in the Scripture where all the members of the Trinity (the Father, Son, and Holy Spirit) are mentioned. In the traditional words of the church the one God exists in three persons but one substance, coeternal and coequal. No amount of explanation can adequately portray the power and intricacy of this unique relationship. There are no perfect analogies in nature because there is no other relationship like the Trinity.

And the Holy Ghost descended in a bodily shape like a dove upon him, and a voice came from heaven, which said, you are my beloved Son, in you I am well pleased (Luke 3 :22).

10. THE COMING OF CHRIST (EXODUS 29:38-43)

<u>God Determined the Requirements of Sacrifice</u>. Every morning and evening, a lamb was sacrificed in the temple for the sins of the people. This was the precursor of Christ through the Old Testament sacrifice in the temple for the sins of the people. The Messiah who is the servant of God would be led to the slaughter

like a lamb. To pay the penalty for sin, a life had to be given and God chose to provide the sacrifice himself.

[38] Now this is that which you shall offer upon the altar; two lambs of the first year day by day continually [39], the one lamb you shall offer in the morning; and the other lamb you shall offer at even: [40] and with the one lamb a tenth deal of flour mingled with the fourth part of a bin of beaten oil; and the fourth part of a bin of wine for a drink offering. [41] And the other lamb you shall offer at even, and shall do thereto according to the meat offering of the morning, and according to the drink offering thereof, for a sweet savor, an offering made by fire unto the Lord. [42] This shall be a continual burnt offering throughout your generations at the door of the tabernacle of the congregation before the Lord where I will meet you to speak there unto you. [43] And there I will meet with the children of Israel, and the tabernacle shall be sanctified by my glory (Exodus 29:38-43).

The Sin of the World. The sins of the world were removed when Jesus died as the perfect sacrifice. This is the way our sins are forgiven. The "sin of the world" means everyone's sin. Jesus paid the price the sin of each individual by His death. You can receive forgiveness by confessing your sin to Him through the repentance of them by confessing to Him and asking for the forgiveness of them.

11. THE MESSIAH: GOD'S SERVANT

The Messiah: God's Servant. This part of the coming of the Messiah is to be studied to help you understand both the Old and New Testament of Jesus Christ. In the Old Testament, people offered animals as sacrifices for their sins. The sinless servant of the Lord offered himself for our sins. He is the Lamb (Isaiah 53:7-12) offered for the sins of all people (John 1:29; Revelation 5:6-14). The Messiah suffered for our sakes, taking our sins to make us acceptable to God. What can we say to such love? How will we respond to him?

Righteous Servant (Isaiah 43:11). "My righteous servant will justify many" tells of the enormous family of believers who will become righteous, not by their own works, but by the Messiah's great work on the cross. They are justified because they have claimed Christ, the righteous servant, as their Savior and Lord (Romans

10:9; 2-Corinthians 5:21). Their life of sin is stripped away and they are clothed with Christ's goodness (Ephesians 4:22-24).

Kingship as Servant of the Lord. Let us go back to the baptism of Jesus at the river of Jordan when the descent of the dove as Jesus came up out of the water was a sign that He was the one anointed by the Spirit of God as the Servant-Messiah of His people (Isaiah 11:2; 61:1). A voice from heaven declared, *You are my beloved Son; in you I am well pleased* (Luke 3:22). This indicated that He was Israel's anointed king, destined to fulfill His kingship as the servant of the Lord described centuries earlier by the prophet (Isaiah 42:1; 52:13).

Temptation in the Wilderness. In the Gospels of Matthew, Mark, and Luke, Jesus' baptism is followed immediately by His temptation in the wilderness (Matthew 4:1-11; Mark 1:12-13; Luke 4:1-13). This test confirmed His understanding of the heavenly voice and His acceptance of the path which it marked out for him. He refused to use His power as God's Son to fulfill His personal desires, to amaze the people, or to dominate the world by political and military force.

CHAPTER 3: WORKSHEET 1
LEARNING ABOUT JESUS (LUKE 2:41-51)

<u>True/False</u>

1. Learning about Jesus according to the law   T / F
    of God in the Old Testament every male
    was required to go to Jerusalem three times
    a year for the great festivals according to
    Deuteronomy 16:16.

2. When Jesus was twelve years old He went to   T / F
    Jerusalem to the Passover.

3. The Passover at Jerusalem was the most   T / F
    important of the three annual festivals
    according to Exodus 12:21-36.

4. Exodus 12:21, Moses said to the people, *Draw*   T / F
    out and take you a lamb according to your family
    and kill the Passover.

5. Jesus' parents went to Jerusalem every year at   T / F
    the feast of the Passover.

6. In Exodus 12:21 *Moses called for all the elders*   T / F
    of Israel, and said unto them, Draw out and take
    you a lamb according to your family, and kill the
    Passover.

7. The boy Jesus went to the temple in Jerusalem.   T / F

8. After a day's journey Jesus' parents could   T / F
    not find their child in the group traveling
    together. The parents thought He was in the
    temple.

9. When Jesus was twelve years old his parents   T / F
    went to the Passover because it was a law
    of God.

10   Luke 2:42 says that when Jesus was twelve   T / F
      years old he went up to Jerusalem with his
      parents.

11.   Luke 2:42 says that when Jesus was twelve   T / F
      years old they went up to Jerusalem after the
      custom of the feast.

12.   Jesus' parents looked for him in the company   T / F
      of his kinsfolk after a day journey.

13.   Jesus' parents returned to Jerusalem looking   T / F
      for Jesus.

14.   Jesus' parents found him with his kinsfolk.   T / F

CHAPTER 3: WORKSHEET 2
LEARNING ABOUT JESUS (LUKE 2:41-51)

<u>True/False</u>

1. Jesus' parents learned that Jesus was in the temple sitting with the sick and unhealthy people.   T / F

2. Luke 2:46. *And it came to pass, that after three days Jesus' parents found the baby child in the midst of the people.*   T / F

3. Luke 2:46. *After the three days they found him in the* _____, *sitting in the midst of the doctors, both hearing them, and asking them questions.*

4. After Jesus increased in wisdom and stature he was able to tell God what to do and how to do it.   T / F

5. When Jesus' parents found him, Jesus shouted angrily at them, *Why did you look for me; didn't you know I was about my Father's business.*   T / F

6. *When Jesus' parents found him, He said unto them how is it that you looked for me? Did you not know I must be about my* _____*business?*

7. Luke 2: Verse _____. Jesus' mother understand the sayings of her son.   T / F

8. Deuteronomy 16:17 says that *every man shall give as he is able, according to the blessing of the Lord your God he has given you.*   T / F

9. Mark 12: Verse _____. *This was the Lord's doing, and it was* _____ *in our eyes, was it told what was done.*   T / F

10. Isaiah 53:7. *The sinless* _____*servant of the Lord offered himself for our sins.*   T / F

11. Isaiah 53:7. *He was oppressed and afflicted.*   T / F

12. John 1:29. *The next day John saw Jesus coming   T / F
    unto him, and said, behold the Lamb of God, which
    take away the sin of the world.*

13. Revelation 5:6. *And I beheld, and, Lo, in the mist
    of the throne and of the four beast, and in the midst
    of the elders, stood a* _____ *as
    it had been slain.*

14. Revelation 5:6. *Having seven horns and seven   T / F
    eyes, which are the seven Spirits of God sent forth
    into all the earth.*

CHAPTER 3: WORKSHEET 3
CONFESSING WITH YOUR MOUTH
(ROMANS 10:9)

True/False

1. a. Confession with your mouth only save you.
   b. Book _____ Chapter_____   T / F
   Verse_____

2. Romans 10:9. *If you shall confess with your mouth*   T / F
   the Lord Jesus, you shall believe in your heart that
   God has raised him from the dead, you shall be
   saved.

3. You can receive SALVATION without   T / F
   repentance.

4. You can be saved by only believing and   T / F
   without having repentance.

5. You can be ignorant of God's Word and   T / F
   receive salvation.

6. Salvation will come by God in repentance   T / F
   through Jesus Christ.

7. Salvation comes by repenting and asking   T / F
   for the forgiveness of your sins with the
   confession to Jesus Christ. Only then will you
   receive forgiveness and be saved.

8. Acts 17:30. *The time of this ignorance God winked*   T / F
   at; but now commands all men everywhere to
   repent.

9. 2-Corinthians 5:21. *The life of sin is stripped*   T / F
   away.

10 God has made Christ to be sin for us, who   T / F
    knew no sin that we might be made the
    righteousness of God through our Lord Jesus
    Christ.

11. Isaiah 11:2 says, *The Spirit of the Lord shall rest*   T / F
     upon him,
     the Spirit of _____ *and understanding,*
     the Spirit of _____ *and might,*
     the Spirit of _____ *and of the fear of*
     the Lord.

12. Isaiah 42:1. *Behold my servant, whom I uphold;*   T / F
     mine elect, in whom my soul delight; I have put
     my spirit upon him: he shall bring forth judgment
     to the Gentiles.

13. Isaiah 61:1. *The Spirit of the Lord God is upon*   T / F
     me; because the Lord have anointed me to preach
     god tidings unto the meek; he have sent me to bind
     up the brokenhearted, to proclaim liberty to the
     captives and the opening of the prison to them that
     are bound.

CHAPTER 3: WORKSHEET 4
(MARK 4:1-11)

<u>True/False</u>

1. Mark 4. Jesus taught many things while   T / F
    standing by the sea side.

2. Mark 4:1 is the parable of the sower.   T / F

3. In Mark 4:1 Jesus taught that some of the seeds   T / F
    that were sowed fell by the way side, and the
    fowls of the air came and devoured it.

4. In Mark 4 it was not actually seed but rather   T / F
    the Word of God.

5. When Jesus was alone the twelve came and
    asked him the meaning of the parable. This
    occurred in Mark 4:1-11_____ or Mark
    4:11-20_____.

6. In Mark 4:20 Jesus said *these are they which are*   T / F
    sown on good ground; such as hear the word, and
    receive it, and bring forth fruit, some thirty fold,
    some sixty, and some a hundred.

7. Satan takes the word from you.   T / F

8. Mark 4:6. *When the sun was up, it was scorched;*   T / F
    and because it had no root, it withered away.

9. Mark 4: 15. *These are they by the way side, where*   T / F
    the word is sown; but when they have heard,
    _____ *came immediately, and*
    took away the word that was sown in their hearts.

10 Jesus was led by the Spirit into the wilderness.   T / F

11. Jesus being full of the Holy Ghost when he   T / F
    returned from Jordan after being baptized by
    John the Baptist.

12. While being tempted by the devil, Jesus ate   T / F
    whatever he wanted.

13. The devil said to Jesus, *If you be the Son of God,*   T / F
    come out of the wilderness and be with me.

14. The devil said, *If you be the Son of God, command*   T / F
    this stone that it be made bread.

CHAPTER 4.
THE KINGDOM OF
GOD IN PROPHECY

1. THE GOSPEL OF THE KINGDOM OF GOD

<u>Time is Fulfilled</u>. Jesus ministered for a very short time in southern and central Palestine while John the Baptist was still preaching. The main phase of Jesus' ministry began in Galilee after John's imprisonment by Herod Antipas. According to Mark's writings, this was the signal for Jesus to proclaim God's News in Galilee: *The time is fulfilled, and the kingdom of God is at hand, repent, and believe in the gospel.*

<u>The Words of Jesus Were the Words of God</u>. John was fully satisfied with the place and work assigned to him. Jesus came to do a more important work. John knew that Jesus would increase in honor and influence. For His government and peace there would be no end, while John would be less followed. John knew that Jesus came from heaven as the Son of God whereas John was a sinful, mortal man, who could only speak about the more plain subjects of religion. The words of Jesus were the words of God; He had the Spirit not by measure as the prophets but in all fullness.

<u>The Popular View of the Kingdom of God</u>. Everlasting life can only be secured by faith in Jesus; whereas all those who believe not in the Son of God, cannot partake of salvation, but the wrath of God forever rests upon them. What is the character of this kingdom? How was it to be established? There is a popular view that the kingdom of God meant throwing off the oppressive yoke of Rome and establishing an independent state of Israel.

After these things came Jesus and his disciples into the land of Judaea; and there he tarried with them, and baptized. And John also was baptizing in

Aenon near to Salim because there was much water there: and they came, and were baptized. For John was not yet cast into prison (John 3:22-24).

The Good News of God. Mark tells dramatic, action packed stories and gives the account of Christ's activities. Rather than Jesus' teachings, Mark features facts and actions about the way Jesus lived His life as the perfect example of how we should live ours today.

What is the Good News of God? These words of Jesus recorded by Mark give the core of His mission: *The long awaited Messiah has come to break the power of sin and begin God's personal reign on earth.* Most of the people who heard this message were the oppressed, poor, and without hope. Jesus' words were the good news because they offered freedom, justice and hope.

*Now after that John was put in prison, Jesus came into Galilee, preaching the gospel of the kingdom of God. And saying, **the time is fulfilled, and the kingdom of God is at hand: repent ye, and believe the gospel*** (Mark 1:14-15).

A Harmony of the Gospels. The entire thirteenth chapter of Mark describes how we are to live while we wait for Christ's return.

- We are not to be misled by confusing claims or speculative interpretations of what will happen (Mark 13:5-6).

- We should not be afraid to tell people about Christ, despite what they might say or do to us (Mark 13 :9-11).

- We must stand firm by faith and not be surprised by persecution (Mark 13:13).

- We must be morally alert, obedient to the commandments for living found in God's Words.

2. SIGNS OF CHRIST'S RETURN (MARK 13:5-6)

Signs of The End Times? There have been people in every generation since Christ's resurrection claiming to know exactly when Jesus would return. No one has been right yet because Christ will return on God's time table not ours. Jesus predicted that before His return, many believers would be misled by teachers claiming to have the revelation from God.

And Jesus began to say to them, **See to it that no one misleads you. Many will come in my name, saying, 'I am He!' and will mislead** (Mark 13:5-6).

Jesus will Appear in the Clouds. According to the Scripture, the one clear sign of Christ's return will be His unmistakable appearance in the clouds, which will be seen by all people (Mark 13 :26 and Revelation 1:7). In other words, you do not have to wonder whether a certain person is the Messiah or whether there is the "end time." When Jesus returns, you will know beyond a doubt, because it will be evident to all. Beware of groups who claim special knowledge of the last days, because no one knows when that time will be (Mark 13:32). Be cautious about anyone saying, "This is it!" Be bold in your total commitment to have your heart and life ready for Christ's return.

Persecution of Christians in the Early Church. As we read references and look back into how the early church began to grow, most of the disciples experienced the kind of persecution Jesus was talking about. Since the time of Christ, Christians have been persecuted in their own land and on foreign mission fields. Although you may be safe from persecution now, your vision of God's kingdom must not be limited by what happens not only to you.

But be on your guard; for they will deliver you to the courts, and you will be flogged in the synagogues, and you will stand before governors and kings for my sake, as a testimony to them. And the gospel must first be preached to all nations (Mark 13:9-10).

And when they arrest you and deliver you up, do not be anxious beforehand about what you are to say, but say whatever is given you in that hour, for it is not you who speak, but it is the Holy Spirit (Mark 13:11).

<u>Christians Facing Hardship and Persecution</u>. The newspaper will reveal that many Christians in other parts of the world daily face hardships and persecution. Persecutions are an opportunity for Christians to witness for Christ to those opposed to them. These persecutions serve God's desire that the gospel be proclaimed to everyone.

And you will be hated by all on account of my name, but the one who endures to the end, he shall be saved (Mark 13: 13).

Therefore, be on the alert for you do not know when the master of the house is coming, whether in the evening, at midnight, at cockcrowing, or in the morning. Lest He come suddenly and find you asleep. And what I say to you I say to all, 'Be on the alert!' (Mark 13:35-37).

3. OLIVET DISCOURSE

Mark 13 is often called the Olivet Discourse. Jesus talked a lot about two things: the end times and His second corning. Jesus was not trying to encourage His disciples to speculate about exactly when He would return by sharing these prophecies with them. Instead, He urged all His followers to be watchful and prepared for His return. If we serve Jesus faithfully now, we will be ready when He returns.

TYPE OF PROPHECY	OLD TESTAMENT REFERENCES	NEW TESTAMENT REFERENCES
THE LAST DAYS	Daniel 9:26-27 Daniel 11:31 Joel 2:2	Mark 13:1-23 Matthew 24:1-28 Luke 21:5-24 = = = = = = = = = = = = John 15:21 Revelation 11:2 1-Timothy 4:12

THE SECOND COMING OF CHRIST		Mark 13:24-27 Luke 21:25-28 Matthew 24:29-31 = = = = = = = = = = = = Revelation 6:12 Mark 14:62 1-Thessalonians 4:16

4. THE DESECRATION OF THE TEMPLE

The Messiah, the Anointed One, will be rejected and killed by His own people. His perfect eternal kingdom will come later (Daniel 9:26-27).

His Perfect Eternal Kingdom Will Come. There has been much discussion on the numbers, times and events in the scriptures. There are three basic views:

(1) The prophecy was fulfilled in the past at the desecration of the temple by Antiochus IV Epiphanes in 168-167 B.C.
(2) It also was fulfilled in the past at the destruction of the temple by the Roman general Titus in A.D. 70 when one million Jews were killed.
(3) It is still to be fulfilled in the future under the antichrist.

And after threescore and two weeks shall Messiah be cut off, but not for himself: and the people of the prince that shall come shall destroy the city and the sanctuary and the end thereof shall be with a flood, And unto the end of the war desolation are determined (Daniel 9:26).

Daniel's Prediction Came True. Antiochus IV would again invade "the South," but enemy ships would cause him to retreat. On his way back, he plundered Jerusalem, desecrated the temple, and stopped the Jews' daily sacrifice. The temple was desecrated when he sacrificed pigs on an altar erected in honor of Zeus. According to Jewish law, pigs were unclean and were not to be touched or eaten. To sacrifice a pig in the temple was the worst kind of insult an enemy could level against the Jews. This happened in 168-167 B.C.

And he shall confirm the covenant with many for one week: and in the midst of the week he shall cause the sacrifice and the oblation to cease. And for the overspreading of abominations he shall make it desolate, even until the consummation, and that determined shall be poured upon the desolate (Daniel 9:27).

And arms shall stand on his part, and they shall pollute the sanctuary of strength, and shall take away the daily sacrifice and they shall place the abomination that make desolate (Daniel 11:31).

<u>Jesus' Words Were Remembered</u>. Jesus' words were remembered in A. D. 70 when Titus placed an idol on the site of the burned temple after destroying Jerusalem. In the end time the antichrist will set up an image of himself and order everyone to worship it. These are all "abominations" that mock God.

When you therefore shall see the abomination of desolation, spoken of by Daniel the prophet stand in the holy place. Whoso read, let him understand. Then let them which be in Judaea flee into the mountains: Let him which is on the housetop: not come down to take anything out of his house (Matthew 24:15-16).

Who oppose and exalt himself above all that is called God or that is worshipped, so that he as God sit in the temple of God showing himself that he is God (2-Thessalonians 2:4).

5. OLD TESTAMENT PREDICTIONS OF END TIMES

<u>Counterfeit Miracles Will Be Performed</u>. Throughout the Bible we see miracles performed as proof of God's power, love, and authority. But there will also be counterfeit miracles performed to deceive. This is a reminder of Pharaoh's magicians, who duplicated Moses' signs in Egypt. True signs and miracles point us to Jesus Christ, but miracles alone can be deceptive. That is why we must ask with respect to each miracle we see: is it consistent with what God says in the Bible?

<u>The Second Beast</u>. The second beast gains influence through the signs and wonders that he can perform on behalf of the first beast. The second beast ordered the people to worship an image in honor of the first beast a direct flouting of the second commandment (Revelation 13:14). We are commanded that we are not to make any image or likeness of anything that is in heaven above, or that is in the earth beneath (Exodus 20:4).

<u>Joel's Indication of Judgment</u>. In Deuteronomy God is contending with His own professing people for their sins and executing upon them the judgment written in the law. The fruit of the land shall the locust consume, which was one of those diseases of Egypt that God would bring upon them. *The cricket shall possess all your trees and the produce of your ground* (Deuteronomy 28:42).

<u>A Day of Darkness</u> (Joel 2:2).
A day of darkness and of gloominess, a day of clouds and of thick darkness, as the morning spreads upon the mountains: a great people and a strong, there hath not been ever the like, neither shall be any more after it, even to the years of many generation.

<u>The War Proclaimed</u> (Joel 2:1). Blow the trumpet in Zion, which means to either call the invading army together, and then the trumpet sounds a charge, or rather to give notice to Judah and Jerusalem of the approach of the judgment, that they might prepare to meet their God in the way of His judgment, that they might endeavor by prayers and tears, the church's best artillery, to put by the stroke.

<u>The Priests Will Sound the Trumpet</u>. It was the priests' responsibility to sound the trumpet.

And the son of Aaron, the priests, shall blow with the trumpet; and they shall be to you for an ordinance forever throughout your generations (Numbers 10:8).

This was an appeal to God in the day of their distress and a summons to the people to come together to seek His face. It is the work of the ministers to give warning from the word of God of the fatal consequences of sin, and to reveal His wrath from heaven against the ungodliness and unrighteousness of men.

<u>Warned But Not Exempt from Judgment</u>. It is not the privilege of Zion and Jerusalem to be exempted from the judgments of God if they provoke him, yet it is their privilege to be warned of them that they might make their peace with God. Even in the holy mountain the alarm must be sounded, and then it sounds must dreadful.

You only have I known of all the families of the earth: Therefore I will punish you for all your iniquities (Amos 3:2).

<u>A Trumpet Shall Be Blown in the Holy City</u>. Now shall a trumpet be blown in the holy city and the people not be afraid? Surely they will. Let all the inhabitants of the land tremble. They shall be made to tremble by the judgment itself. Let them therefore tremble at the alarm of it.

Shall a trumpet be blown in the city, and the people not be afraid? Shall there be evil in a city, and the Lord hath not done it? (Amos 3:6).

<u>The Day of Battle and Judgment</u>. A general idea is given of the day of battle to come and there is no avoiding it. It is the day of the Lord, the day of His judgment, in which He will both manifest and magnify himself. It is a day of darkness and gloominess (Joel 2:2). It warns of locusts and caterpillars. I was working at NIH at the time locusts came through Bethesda, Maryland. They got into houses and cars and anything that was open that they could fly into. It was like a dark cloud passing over. It was something to see. Read Exodus 10:15.

6. THE DOOM OF BABYLON (ISAIAH 13:6-10)

<u>The Day of the Lord is Near</u>. This is a vivid description of the terrible confusion and desolation which should be made in Babylon by the descent which the Medes and the Persians should make upon it. Those who were now secure and easy were bidden to howl and make sad lamentation for God was about to appear in

wrath against them, and it is a fearful thing to fall into His hands: the day of the Lord is at hand.

Wail, for the day of the Lord is near! It will come as destruction from the Almighty (Isaiah 13:6).

<u>God Will Act as a Just Avenger</u>. A day of judgment when God will act as a just avenger of His own and His people's injured cause. And there are those who will have reason to tremble when that day is at hand. The day of the Lord will come.

Behold, the day of the Lord is coming, Cruel, with fury and burning anger, to make the land a desolation; and He will exterminate its sinners from it (Isaiah 13:9).

<u>Men Have Their Day Now</u>. Men have their day now, and they think to carry the day; but God pities them, for He sees that His day of reckoning with the Babylonians is said to be cruel with wrath and fierce anger.

The Lord shall laugh at him: for He sees that His day is coming (Psalm 37:13).

Their hearts shall fail them, and they shall have neither courage nor comfort left; they shall not be able either to resist the judgment coming or to bear up under it, either to oppose the enemy or to support themselves.

Therefore shall all hands be faint, and every man's heart shall melt: and they shall be afraid: Pangs and sorrows shall take hold of them; they shall be in pain as a woman that travail: They shall be amazed one at another; their faces shall be as flames (Isaiah 13:7).

Those that are in the day of their peace were proud, and haughty, and terrible,

And I will punish the world for their evil, and the wicked for their iniquity, and I will cause the arrogance of the proud to cease, and will lay low the haughtiness of the terrible (Isaiah 13:11).

In frightening themselves, they shall frighten one another, they shall wonder to see those that used to be bold and daring; or they shall be amazed looking one at the other, as men at a loss.

Now when Jacob saw that there was corn in Egypt, Jacob said unto his son, why do you look one upon another? (Genesis 42:1).

Faces Will Be As Flames. Their faces shall be as flames, pale as flames, through fear, some are red as flames some are blushing at their own cowardice; or their faces shall be as faces scorched with the flame or as theirs that labor in the fire, their visage blacker than a coal, or like a bottle in the smoke.

All Comfort and Hope Shall Fail.
For I am become like a bottle in the smoke; yet do I not forget they statues. All comfort and hope shall fail them (Psalm 119:83).

The Stars of Heaven Shall Fail. The stars of heaven shall not give their light, but shall be clouded and overcast. The sun shall be darkened in his going forth, rising bright, but lost again, a certain sign of foul weather.

The Displeasure of the God of Heaven. They shall be as men in distress at sea, when neither sun nor stars appear. It shall be as dreadful a time with them as it would be with the earth if all the heavenly luminaries were turned into darkness, a resemblance of the day of judgment, when the sun shall be turned into darkness. The heavens frowning thus is an indication of the displeasure of the God of heaven. When things look dark on earth, yet it is well enough if all be clear upwards, but if we have no comfort wherewith shall we be comforted?

And when neither sun nor stars in many days appeared, and no small tempest lay on us, all hope that we should be saved was then taken away (Acts 27:20).

Wormwood and Gall (Isaiah 13:11). God will visit them for their iniquity. All this is intended for the punishment of sin, and particularly the sin of pride.

And I will punish the world for their evil, and the wicked for their iniquity; and I will cause the arrogance of the proud to cease, and will lay the haughtiness of the terrible (Isaiah 13:11).

<u>Affliction and Misery</u>. This puts wormwood and gall into the affliction and misery, that sin must now have its punishment. Though Babylon be a little world, yet being a wicked one, it shall not go unpunished. Sin brings desolation on the world of the ungodly. When the kingdoms of the earth are quarrelling with one another it is the fruit of God's controversy with them all that pride must now have its fall. The haughtiness of the terrible must now be laid low, particularly of Nebuchadnezzar and his son Belshazzar who had in their pride trampled upon and made themselves very terrible to the people of God. A man's pride will bring him low.

<u>Universal Confusion</u>. Such a confusion of their affairs that it shall be like the shaking of the heavens with dreadful thunders and the moving of the earth by no less dreadful earthquakes, All shall go to rack and ruin in the day of the wrath of the Lord of hosts.

Therefore I will shake the heavens, and the earth shall remove out of her place, in the wrath of the Lord of hosts, and in the day of His fierce anger (Isaiah 13:13).

And such a consternation shall seize their spirit that Babylon, which used to be like a roaring lion and a raging bear to all about her, shall become as a chased roe and as a sheep that no man takes up.

And it shall be as the chased roe, and as a sheep that no men take up. They shall every man turn to his own people, and flee every one into his own land (Isaiah 13:14).

It is dangerous being in bad company, and helping those whom God is about to destroy. Those particularly that join themselves to Babylon must expect to share in her plagues.

And I heard another voice from heaven, saying, Come out of her, my people, that you be not partakers of her sin, and that you receive not of her plagues (Revelation 18:4).

<u>Wickedness Would Have Free Reign</u>. Since the most sacred laws of nature and of humanity are silenced by the fury of war, the conquerors shall act in the most barbarous brutish manner. In other words there is a lack of reason or intelligence. Wickedness shall have free reign.

It was foretold that the little ones of Babylon should be dashed against the stone. How cruel and unjust were they who did it. God was righteous who suffered it to be done, and to be done before their eyes to their greater terror and vexation. It was also just that the house which they had filled with the spoils of Israel should be spoiled and plundered.

Their children also shall be dashed to pieces before their eyes; Their houses shall be spoiled, and their wives ravished (Isaiah 13: 16).

Happy shall he be who takes and dashes your little ones against the stone (Psalm 137:9).

They had just dealt with God's people:

They ravished the women in Zion, and the maids in the cities of Judah (Lament 5:11).

And now they shall be paid in their own coin.

He that leaded into captivity shall go into captivity: He that killed with the sword must be killed with the sword (Revelation 13:10).

<u>Vengeance Belongs to God</u>. The men whould be cruel and inhuman, and so utterly divested of all compassion; and in it see how corrupt and degenerate the nature of man has become. The God of infinite mercy should suffer it and should make it to be the execution of His justice, which shows that He is gracious, yet He is the God to whom vengeance belongs.

7. DESTRUCTION OF EGYPT

<u>Lamentation for Pharaoh King of Egypt</u> (Ezekiel 32:1-16). The prophet was ordered to take up a lamentation for Pharaoh, King

of Egypt. It concerns ministers to be of a serious spirit. In order to take up lamentation for the fall and ruin of sinners who have not desired, but instead have dreaded the woeful day. Ministers who influence others while serving God must repent themselves of their sins. It becomes us to weep and tremble for those who will not weep and tremble for themselves, by our example setting them a weeping and trembling. God ordered this to show cause for that lamentation. Pharaoh has been a troubler of the nation, even of His own nation, which He should have procured the repose of. He is like a young lion of the nations.

Son of man take up a lamentation for Pharaoh king of Egypt, and say you are as a whale in the seas: and you came forth with your rivers, and troubled the waters with your feet, and fouled their rivers (Ezekiel 32:1-16).

<u>Pharaoh Warred Against Cyrenia</u>. When Pharaoh engaged in an unnecessary war with the Cyrenians he came forth with his armies which disturbed his own kingdom and the neighboring nations, fouled the rivers and made them muddy. A great deal of disquiet is often given to the world by the restless ambition and implacable resentment of proud princes. Ahab troubled Israel and not Elijah. He who troubles others must expect to be himself troubled for the Lord is righteous.

And Joshua said, *Why have you troubled us? The Lord shall trouble you this day, and all Israel stoned Him with stones, and burned them with fire, after they had stoned them with stones* (Joshua 7:15).

Is Pharaoh like a great whale, in which He comes up out of the river, gives great disturbance, a leviathan which Job cannot draw out with a hook?

Cast your draw out leviathan with an hook? Or His tongue with a cord which you let down (Job 41:1).

Yet God has a net for Him which is large enough to enclose Him and strong enough to secure Him (Ezekiel 32:3).

<u>Pharaoh Defeated Like a Netted Fish</u>. I will spread my net over you, even the army of the Chaldeans, a company of many people. They shall force him out of his fastnesses, dislodge him out of his possessions, and throw him like a great fish upon dry ground upon the open field.

Then will I leave you upon the land. I will cast you forth upon the open field, and will cause all the fowls of the heaven to remain upon you, and will fill the beasts of the whole earth with you (Ezekiel 32:4).

<u>Pharaoh Attacked by His Enemies</u>. Where being out of his element he must die of course and be a prey to the birds and beasts, as it was foretold.

And I will leave you thrown into the wilderness, you and all the fish of your rivers. You shall fall upon the open fields. You shall not be brought together, nor gathered. I have given you for meat to the beasts of the field and to the fowls of the heaven (Ezekiel 29:5).

<u>Pharaoh Will Be Helpless</u>. What can the strongest fish do to help itself when it is out of the water and lies gasping? The flesh of this great whale shall be laid upon the mountains.

And I will lay your flesh upon the mountains, and fill the valleys with your height (Ezekiel 32:5).

<u>Many Soldiers Will Die and Lay Unburied</u>. Such numbers of Pharaoh's soldiers shall be slain that the dead bodies shall be scattered upon the hills and there shall be heaps of them piled up in the valleys. Blood shall be shed in such abundance as to swell the rivers in the valleys. Such shall be the bulk and the height of this leviathan that when he is laid upon the ground, he shall fill a valley. Such vast quantities of blood shall issue from this leviathan as shall water the land of Egypt, the land wherein now he swims, now he sports himself.

I will also water with your blood the land wherein you swim, even to the mountains; and the rivers shall be full of you (Ezekiel 32:6)

<u>Vast Quantities of Blood from the Battlefield Will Flow Into the Rivers</u>. It shall reach to the mountains, and the waters of Egypt shall again be turned into blood. The rivers shall be full of it. The judgment executed upon Pharaoh of old are expressed by the breaking of the hands of leviathan in the waters. But now they go further, this old serpent not only has now his head bruised but is all crushed to pieces.

Thus did divide the sea by your strength. You brake the head of the dragons in the water. You brake the head of leviathan in pieces, and gave him to be meat to the people inhabiting the wilderness (Psalm 74:13-14).

<u>The Destruction of Egypt Prophesized by Ezekiel</u>. It is set forth by a prophecy of the deep impression which the destruction of Egypt should make upon the neighboring nation. It would put them all into a consternation, as the fall of the Assyrian monarchy did.

Thus said the Lord God; in the day when he went down to the grave I caused mourning. I covered the deep for him, and I restrained the floods thereof, and the great waters were stayed and I caused Lebanon to mourn for him, and all the trees of the field fainted for him. I made the nations to shake at the sound of his fall, when I cast him down to hell with them that descend into the pit. And all the trees of Eden, the choice and best of Lebanon, all that drink water, shall be comforted in the nether parts of the earth (Ezekiel 31:15-16).

When Pharaoh, who had been like a blazing burning torch that has been extinguished shall be blackened all around him.

And when I shall put you out, I will cover the heaven, and make the stars thereof dark. I will cover the sun with a cloud, and the moon shall not give her light (Ezekiel 32:7).

<u>There Will be Only Darkness in the Heavens</u>. The heavens shall be hung with black, the stars darkened, the sun eclipsed, and the moon be deprived of her borrowed light. It is from the upper world that this lower receives its light.

All the bright light of heaven will I make over you and set darkness upon your land, said the Lord God (Ezekiel 32:8).

<u>The Land of Egypt will be Dark for Three Days</u>. When the bright lights of heaven are made dark above, darkness by consequence is set upon the land, upon the earth; so it shall be on the land of Egypt of old for three days, seems to be alluded to, as before, the turning of the waters into blood.

<u>Mankind Will Repeat the Mistakes of the Past</u>. For when former judgments are forgotten it is just that they should be repeated. When their privy counselors and statesmen and those who have the direction of the public affairs are deprived of wisdom and made fools and the things that belong to their peace are hidden from their eyes, then their lights are darkened and the land is in a mist. This is foretold.

The princes of Zion are become fools, the princes of Nosh are deceived; they have also seduced Egypt, even they that are the stay of the tribes thereof (Isaiah 19:13).

<u>Babylon Will Defeat Egypt</u>. It is set forth a plain and express prediction of the instruments of the desolation appear here very formidable. It is the sword of the king of Babylon, that warlike, that victorious prince, that shall come upon you. The swords of the mighty, even the terrible of the nations, all of them in an army that there is no standing before.

For this said the Lord God; the sword of the King of Babylon shall come upon you. [12] By the swords of the mighty will I cause the multitude to fall, the terrible of the nations, all of them; and they shall spoil the pomp of Egypt, and the multitude thereof shall be destroyed (Ezekiel 32:11-12).

<u>Nations Who Have Turned From God Will be made Destitute</u>. The Egyptians were full of their pleasant and plentiful country, and its rich production. Every one that talked with them might perceive how much it filled them. But God can soon make their country destitute of that whereof it is full. It is therefore our wisdom to be full of treasures in heaven. When the country is made destitute, it shall be an instruction to them. Then shall they know that I am the Lord. A sensible conviction of the vanity of the world, and the

81

fading perishing nature of all things in it, will contribute much to our right knowledge of God as our portion and happiness.

<u>The Daughters of the Nations Shall Lament Their Downfall</u>. It shall be a lamentation to all about them. The daughters of the nations shall lament her, either because, being in alliance with her, they share in her grievance and suffer with her; being admirers of her they at least share in her grief and sympathize with her. They shall lament for Egypt and all her multitude. It shall excite their pity to see to so great a devastation made. By enlarging the matters of our joy we increase the occasions of our sorrow.

This is the lamentation wherewith they shall lament her. The daughters of the nations shall lament her. They shall lament her for her, even for Egypt, and for all her multitude, said the Lord God (Ezekiel 32:16).

8. THE DIVINE KING

<u>The Clouds of Heaven Portray the Son of Man as Divine</u>. Throughout the Bible clouds represent His majesty and awesome presence. Daniel is given visions throughout the night that behold the Son of man coming with the clouds of heaven and came to the Ancient days, and they brought Him near before Him (Daniel 7:13-14).

This "one like a son of man" is the Messiah. Jesus used this verse to refer to himself. The clouds of heaven portray the Son of Man as divine. Throughout the Bible clouds represent His majesty and awesome presence.

<u>Old Testament</u>

- This one like a son of man is the Messiah Jesus used this verse to refer to himself (Daniel 7:13-14)

- God's glory appeared in the cloud (Exodus 16:10)

- And at Mt. Sinai the law (Exodus 19:9)

New Testament

- Jesus referred to himself (Matthew 26:64; Luke 21:27; John 1:15)

Jesus Declared His Royalty. Jesus declared His royalty in no uncertain terms. Saying He was the Son of Man, Jesus was claiming to be the Messiah as His listeners well knew. He knew His declaration would be His undoing, but He did not panic. He was calm, courageous, and determined.

Jesus said unto him, **Thou has said: Nevertheless I say unto you, hereafter shall you see the Son of Man sitting on the right hand of power, and coming in the clouds of heaven** (Matthew 26:64).

The World Hated the Disciples for Belonging to Christ. This was the core cause of the controversy. Whatever is pretended this was the grounds of the quarrel. They hated Christ's disciples because they bore His name and bore up His name in the world.

Another cause of the world's hating you will be because you do belong to Christ, for my name's sake (John 15:21).

Those Who Stand for Christ May Suffer. It is the character of Christ's disciples that they stand up for His name. The name into which they were baptized is that which they will live and die by. It has commonly been the lot of those who appear for Christ's name to suffer for doing so. Yet it is a matter of comfort to the greatest sufferers that they suffer for Christ's name's sake. If you be reproached for the name of Christ, happy are you.

If you be reproached for the name of Christ, happy are you; for the spirit of glory and of God rest upon you: on their part He is evil spoken of, but on your part He is glorified (1-Peter 4:14).

Christ discusses hatred, which is the character and genius of the kingdom of evil, and the opposite of love which is the kingdom of Christ. Who are they in whom this hatred is found in the world?

- The children of this world, as distinguished from the children of God;

- Those who are in the interests of the god of this world, whose image they bear, and whose power they are subject to; and

- All those, whether Jews or Gentiles, who would not come into the church of Christ, which He audibly called and visibly separates from this evil world.

But all these things will they do unto you for my name's sake, because they know not Him that sent me. If I had not come and spoken unto them, they would not have sin: but now that they have no cloak for their sin. He that hates me hates my Father also. If I had not done among them the works which other men did, who had not had sin: but now they have both seen and hated both me and my Father. But this must come to pass, that the word might be fulfilled that is written in their law, they hated me without a cause (John 15:21-25).

<u>Christians Spiritually Protected</u>. Those who worship inside the temple will be protected spiritually, but those outside will face great suffering. This means that true believers will be protected through persecution, but those who refuse to believe will be destroyed.

But the crowd which is without the temple leave out, and measure it not; for it is given into the Gentiles: and the holy city shall they tread under foot forty and two months (Revelation 11:2).

<u>Some Will Depart from the Faith</u>. The "later times" began with Christ's resurrection and will continue until His return when He will set up His kingdom and judge all humanity. The Spirit speaks expressly that in the latter times some shall depart from the faith giving heed to seducing spirits and doctrines of devils.

9. THE KEY TO THE KINGDOM

The Key to the Kingdom of Heaven (Matthew 16:19). The meaning of "the key of heaven" has been a subject of debate by Christian leaders for centuries.

- Some think the key represents the authority to carry out church discipline, legislation, and administration.

- Others think the key gives the authority to announce the forgiveness of sins.

- Some believe the key may be the opportunity to bring people to Christ.

The Key Gives Authority to Rule. Some say the key represents the authority to carry out church discipline, legislation, and administration. It has been the subject of debate in the church for centuries.

Moreover if your brother shall trespass against you, go and tell him his fault between you and him alone. If he shall hear you, you have gained your Brother. But if he will not hear you, then take with you one or two more that in the mouth of two or three witnesses every word may be established. And if he should neglect to hear them, tell it unto the church but if he neglect to hear the church, let him be unto you as heathen man and a publican. Verily I say unto you, whatsoever you shall bind on earth shall be bound in heaven: and whatsoever you shall loose on earth shall be loosed in heaven (Mathew 18:15-18).

The Key Gives Authority to Forgive Sin. Others say the key gives the authority to announce the forgiveness of sins.

Whosoever sins you remit, they are remitted unto them; and whosoever sins you retain, they are retained (John 20:23).

Religious Leaders Sought the Key to the Kingdom. The religious leaders thought they held the key to the kingdom and they tried to keep some people out. We cannot decide to open or close the kingdom of heaven for others, but God uses us to help others find the way inside. The religious leaders thought they held the key to heaven or the kingdom, and they tried to shut some people out. To all who believe in Christ and obey His words the kingdom doors are swung wide open. Read Matthew, John and Acts. It was necessary to weave this combination of love Christ showed His Father and to His followers.

The Keys to Bringing People to Christ. This way of thinking is incorrect. It is God's job to bring reconciliation to the people through Christ Jesus. That is the process by which God and man are brought together again. The Bible teaches that God and man are alienated from one another because of God's holiness and man's sinfulness.

10. CHURCH LEADERSHIP

The Word of God is the Key to the Kingdom (Acts 15:7-11). It is the Word of God that leads us to eternal life with Him through our Lord Jesus Christ.

- The church disciplines took the gospel to non-Jewish people (Peter said in Acts 15:7-11)

- Paul and Barnabas disagreed (Acts 15:12)

- What James proposed for this debate, and the letter that was written to the Gentile coverts directing them how to govern themselves with respect to Jews (Acts 15:22-29)

- Delivering this determination to the church at Antioch, and the satisfaction it gave them (Acts 15:30-35)

- A second expedition planned by Paul and Barnabas to preach to the Gentiles during which they quarreled about their assistant and separated because of it, each of them steering a different course (Acts 15:36-41)

Principles for Receiving Eternal Life. When one would like to know what the **key of the kingdom** is about, the principles of receiving eternal life are the same as having the key, which is the Word of God. Jesus said He would build His church upon Peter when Jesus asked Peter, **Who do you say that I am**? And Peter replied, *You are the Christ, the Son of the living God.*

Jesus answered and said unto him, **Blessed art you, Simon Barjona: for flesh and blood have not revealed it unto you, but my Father which is in heaven. And I say also unto you that you art Peter, and upon this (rock) I will build my church, and the gates of hell shall not prevail against it** (Matthew 16:15-18).

No man can come unto me except He who has sent Me drew him, and I will raise Him up the last day (John 6:44).

It is the Word of God which is the key that opens the gates of heaven to everyone who believes in the Son of the living God who is the Father of us all.

<u>False Teachers are a Threat to the Church</u>. False teachers were and still are a threat to the church. Jesus and the apostles repeatedly warned against them (Mark, Acts, and 2- Thessalonians).

<u>Influence of Greek Philosophers</u>. The danger that Timothy faced in Ephesus seems to have come from certain people in the church who were following Greek philosophers who taught that the body was evil and that only the soul mattered. The false teachers did not believe that the God of creation was good, because His very contact with the physical world would have soiled him. The church members influenced by Greek philosophers honored Jesus but did not believe He was truly human.

And if any man shall say to you, Lo, here is Christ; or Lo, He is there, believe him not for false Christs and false prophets shall rise and shall show signs and wonders to seduce, if it were possible, even the elect. But you take heed. Behold, I have foretold you all things (Mark 13:21-23).

Take heed therefore unto yourselves, and to all the flock, over which the Holy Ghost has made you overseers, to feed the church of God, which He had purchased with His own blood. For I know this, that after my departing shall grievous wolves enter in among you, not sparing the flock. Also of your own selves shall men arise, speaking perverse things, to draw away disciples after them. Therefore watch, and remember, that by the space of three years I ceased not to warn every one night and day with tears (Acts 20:28-31).

Be Not Troubled by Spirits, Words or Letters. Do not be deceived by claims that the day of the Lord has come. There will be many who will be deceived and turn from Christ and worship an evil one who calls himself God.

Now we beseech you, brethren, by the coming of our Lord Jesus Christ, and by our gathering together unto him, that you be not soon shaken in mind, or be troubled, neither by spirit, nor by word, nor by letters as from us, as that the day of Christ is at hand, let no man deceive you by any means: for that day shall not come, except there come a falling away first and that man of sin be revealed, the son of perdition; who oppose and exalt himself above all that is called God, or that is worshipped; so that he as God sit in the temple of God, showing himself that he is God (1-Timothy 4:1-2).

The Physical World. Of all people, the high priest and members of the Sanhedrin should have recognized the Messiah because they knew the Scripture thoroughly. Their job was to point people to God, but they were more concerned about preserving their reputation and holding onto their authority. They valued human security, power, and wealth more than eternal security.

Knowing this first, that there shall come in the last days scoffers, walking after their own lusts, and saying, where is the promise of His coming? For since the fathers fell asleep, all things continue as they were from the beginning of the creation; For this they willingly are ignorant of, that by the word of God the heavens were of old and the earth standing out of the water and in the water, whereby the world that then was, being overflowed with water perished: But the heavens and the earth which are now by the same word are kept in store, reserved unto fire against the day of judgment and perdition of ungodly men (2-Peter 3:3-7).

The Sixth Seal Affects the Physical World. The sixth seal changes the scene back to the physical world. The first five judgments were directed toward specific areas, but this judgment is universal. Everyone will be afraid when the earth itself trembles.

And I behold when he had opened the sixth seal, and, Lo, there was a great earthquake and the sun became black as sackcloth of hair, and the moon became as blood (Revelation 6:12).

To the first question Jesus made no reply because it was based on confusing and erroneous evidence. Not answering was wiser than trying to clarify the fabricated accusations. But if Jesus had refused to answer the second question, it could have been taken as a denial of His mission. Instead, Jesus' answer predicted a powerful role reversal when he answered, *Sitting on the right hand of power, He would come to judge His accusers, and they would have to answer His questions.*

The Lord said unto my Lord, you sit at my right hand until I make your enemies your footstool (A Psalm of David, Psalm 110:1).

[11] And I saw a great white throne, and Him that sat on it from whose face the earth and the heaven fled away, and there was found no place for them. [12] And I saw the dead, small and great, stand before God; and the books were opened. And another book was opened, which is the book of life, and the dead were judged out of those things which were written in the books, according to their works. [13] And the sea gave up the dead which were in it, and death and hell delivered up the dead which were in them, and they were judged every man according to their works (Revelation 20:11-13).

<u>The Lord Will Descend from Heaven</u>. Paul said, *The Lord himself shall descend from heaven.* What does Paul mean when he says, *according to the Lord's own word*? We can take it as something that the Lord had revealed directly to him, passed along orally by the apostles and other Christians.

For the Lord himself shall descend from heaven with a shout, with the voice of the archangel, and with the trump of God: and the dead in Christ shall rise first (1-Thessalonians 4:16).

<u>Take Heed of Doctrine</u>. We know the importance of watching our lives closely. We must be on constant guard against falling into sin that can so easily destroy us. We must watch what we believe ("doctrine") just as closely. Wrong beliefs can quickly lead us into

sin and heresy. We should be on guard against those who would persuade us that how we live is more important than what we believe. We should persevere in both.

Take heed unto yourself, and unto the doctrine, continue in them: for in doing this you shall both save yourself, and them that hear you (1-Timothy 4:16).

11. THE GOOD NEWS MESSAGE FROM JESUS

Mark tells us the dramatic action packed stories of Jesus ministry. He gives us the most vivid account of Christ's activities. Mark features facts and actions rather than teachings. The way Jesus lived His life is the perfect example of how we should live our lives today. Mark 1:14-15 asks the question, *What is the good news of God*? These first words spoken by Jesus and quoted by Mark give the core of His teaching: that the long awaited Messiah has come to break the power of sin and bring God's personal reign on earth.

Now after that John was put in prison, Jesus came into Galilee, preaching the gospel of the kingdom of God, and saying, the time is fulfilled, and the kingdom of God is at hand. Repent you, and believe the gospel (Mark 1: 14-15).

Mark 13 tells us how we must live while we wait for Christ's return:

(1) We are not to be misled by confusing interpretations of what will happen.
(2) We should not be afraid to tell people about Christ, despite what they might say or do to us.
(3) We must stand firm by faith and not be surprised by persecution.
(4) We must be morally alert, obedient to the commands for living found in God's Word.

This chapter does not promote discussions on prophetic timetables, but to stimulate right living for God in a world where He is largely ignored.

Jesus said, **What I say unto you I say unto all: Watch** (Mark 13:37).

CHAPTER 4: WORKSHEET 1
JESUS' PROPHECIES IN THE OLIVET
DISCOURSE
(MARK 13; LUKE 21)

<u>True/False</u>

1. The New Testament prophecies of the last days
    are in
    Mark_____ Matthew _____ Luke _____

2. In Mark 13:9 Jesus was asking his disciples
    to be on their guard because they would be   T / F
    delivered to the courts. WHY: _____
    _____

3. *You will stand before governors and kings for my
    sake.*
    Mark 13:9_____ or Mark 13:35_____

4. Mark 13:35, *Therefore, be on the alert for you do
    not know when the* _____ *of
    the house is coming.*

5. Mark 13 verse _____. *And when they
    arrest you and deliver you up, do not be anxious
    beforehand about what you are to say.*

6. Mark 13 verse 9_____ or 13_____
    *You will be hated by all on account of my name, but
    the one who endures to the end, he shall be_____*
    _____

7. Mark 13:10 says, *And the gospel must first be*   T / F
    *preached to all the nations lest he come suddenly
    and find you asleep.*

8. Mark 13:36, *What I say to you I say to all, 'Be on*   T / F
    the alert!'

9. Luke 21:5-24. The "times of the Gentiles" began   T / F
    with Babylon's destruction of Jerusalem in 586
    B.C. and the exile of the Jewish people. Israel
    was no longer an independent nation but was
    under the control of Gentile rulers.

CHAPTER 4: WORKSHEET 2
TYPE OF PROPHECY (MATTHEW 24; MARK 13)

<u>True/False</u>

1. Although we don't know exactly what the
    temple looked like, it must have been beautiful   T / F
    And Jesus came out from the temple and was
    going away when His disciples came up to
    point out the temple buildings to him.
    This is in the Book of Mark Chapter _____
    Verse_____

2. Matthew 24: verse _____ says, *Do you not see*   T / F
    all these things? Truly I say to you, not one stone
    here shall be left upon another, which will not be
    torn down.

3. Matthew 24:3 says, *And as He was sitting on the*
    Mount of Olives, the _____ came to
    him privately, saying, 'Tell us, when these things
    be, and what will be the sign of your coming, and
    of the end of the age?'

4. Matthew 24:5, *For many will come in my name,*
    saying, I am the _____, and will
    mislead many.

5. Mark 13:1 says, *As Jesus and his disciples were*   T / F
    going up to the temple, one of them said to Jesus,
    'Teacher, behold what wonderful stones and what
    wonderful buildings.'

6. Mark 13:7 says, *And when you hear of wars and*   T / F
    rumors of wars, do not be frightened; those things
    must take place; but that is not yet the end.

7. Mark 13:22 says, *For false Christs and false prophets will arise, and will show signs and wonders, in order, of possible, to lead the elect astray.*   T / F

8. Mark 13:23, Jesus said he had told his disciples everything in advance.   T / F

9. Mark 13:29, *Even so, you too, when you see these things happening, recognize that He is near, tight at the door.*   T / F

CHAPTER 4: WORKSHEET 3
CHRIST'S SECOND COMING (MATTHEW 24; ISAIAH 24)

True/False

1. These verses point to Christ's second coming to judge the world. In their questioning, the disciples had confused the destruction of Jerusalem with the end of the world. In Matthew 24:3 The disciples asked questions concerning the same thing. The only difference is that they did it privately asking _____ when shall these things be?

2. In Matthew 24:4, Jesus said unto them that they   T / F
    must take heed that no man deceive them.

3. Matthew 24: _____ The destruction of Jerusalem which was build upon a mistake, as if the temple must needs stand as long as the world stands. This mistake Christ rectifies, and shows that the end of the world in those days, those other days you enquire about, is the day of Christ's coming, and the day of _____, shall be after that tribulation, and not coincident with it.

4. Book of Isaiah 24 Verse _____Let those who live see the Jewish nation destroyed, take heed of thinking that, because the Son of man do not visibly come in the clouds then, he will never so come; no he will come after that. And here he foretells, the final dissolution of the present frame and fabric of the world; even of that part of it which seems least liable to change, the upper part, the pure and more refined part. The sun shall be darkened, and the moon shall no more give her light; for they shall be quite outshone by the glory of the Son of man.

5. Jesus talked about the glory and reign in   T / F
    Mount Zion, and in Jerusalem, and before his
    ancients gloriously in Isaiah 24:23

CHAPTER 4: WORKSHEET 4
CHRIST'S SECOND COMING
(MATTHEW 13; 1-THESSALONIANS 4)

<u>True/False</u>

1. The stars of heaven, that from the beginning had kept their place and regular notion, shall fall as leaves in autumn; and the powers that are in heaven, the heavenly bodies, the fixed stars, shall be shaken.
Mark 13: _____The visible appearance of the Lord Jesus, to whom the judgment of that day shall be committed.

2. Mark 13 :26 is saying, *And then shall they see the Son of man coming in the* _____*with great power and glory.*

3. It could be the same place where he sat when he said this; for the clouds are in the lower region of the air.   T / F

4. Mark 13: _____ *He shall come with great power and glory, such as will be suited to the errand on which he comes. Every eye shall then see him.*   T / F

5. Mark 13:27 says, *And then shall he send his* _____, *and shall gather his elect from the: four, winds, from the uttermost part of the earth to the uttermost part of heaven*

6. 1-Thessalonians 4: 17, says, *Then we which are*   T / F
   all alive and remain shall be caught up together
   with them in the clouds, to meet the Lord in the air:
   and so shall we ever be with the Lord. This means
   He shall send his angels, and gather together
   to meet him in the air.

7. Book_____ Chapter_____
   Verse_____. *They shall be fetched from*
   one end of the world to the other, so that none
   shall be missing from that great assembly, they
   shall be fetched from the uttermost part of the
   earth, most remote from the places where Christ's
   tribunal shall be set, and shall be brought to the
   uttermost part of heaven; so sure, so swift, so easy,
   shall their conveyance be, that there shall none of
   them miscarry, though they were to be brought
   from the uttermost part of the earth one way, to the
   uttermost part of heaven.

CHAPTER 4: WORKSHEET 5
CHART #5
CONCERNING THE SECOND COMING OF CHRIST

Having given them an idea of the times for about 38 years next ensuing, He comes to show them what all these things would issue in at last, namely, the destruction of Jerusalem, and the utter dispersion of the Jewish nation, which would be a little day of judgment, a type and figure of Christ's second coming, which was not so fully spoken of here as in the parallel place according to Matthew 24. Yet it was glanced at; for the destruction of Jerusalem would be as it were the destruction of the world to those whose heart were bound up in it.

He told them that they whould see Jerusalem besieged, surrounded by armies. This shows how people can misunderstand things concerning the Word of God.

Jesus tells his disciples about his coming. They thought it was about Jerusalem that would be the time of Jesus' coming. Jesus tells them in Luke 21:20-22 about the things they are to be concern about his coming.

And when you shall see Jerusalem compassed with armies, then know that the desolation thereof is nigh (Luke 21:2).

The Roman armies; and, when they saw this, they might conclude that its desolation was nigh, the siege would end, though it might a long siege.

As in mercy, so in judgment, when God begins, he will make an end.

He warns them, upon this signal given, to shift for their own safety. Luke 21:21 says, *Then let them which are in Judea flee to the mountains; and let them which are in the midst if it depart out; and let not them that are in the countries enter there into.*

CHAPTER 4: WORKSHEET 6
CHART#6
THE SECOND COMING OF CHRIST (LUKE 21)

<u>True/False</u>

1.   Jesus foretells the terrible havoc that will cause great harm and destruction of the Jewish nation. Luke 21:22 says, *For these be the days of vengeance, that all things which are written may be fulfilled.*   T / F

2.   REFLECTION:
These are the days of vengeance so often spoken of by the Old Testament prophets, which would complete the ruin of that provoking people. All their predictions must now be fulfilled, and the blood of all the Old Testament martyrs must now be required. All things that are written must be fulfilled at length. After days of patience long abused, there will come days of vengeance; for reprieves are not pardons. The greatness of that destruction is set forth, but the inflicting cause of it. It is wrath upon this people, the wrath of God that will kindle this devouring consuming fire.

Jesus describes the great fear that people should generally be in. Many frightful sights shall be in the sun, moon, and stars, prodigies in the heavens, and here in this lower world, the sea and the waves roaring, with terrible storms and tempests, such as had not been known, and above the ordinary working of natural causes.

The effect of this shall be universal confusion and consternation upon the earth, distress of nations with perplexity, the Jewish nation, Judea, Samaria, and Galilee; these shall be brought to the last extremity.

3.   Luke 21 :25- 26, *[25] Men's hearts failing them for*   T / F
           fear, and for looking after those things which are
           coming upon the earth: for the powers of heaven
           shall be shaken. [26] And then shall they see the
           Son of man coming in a cloud with power and
           great glory

CHAPTER 4: WORKSHEET 7
CHART# 7
CONCERNING THE SECOND COMING OF CHRIST
(ROMANS 8; ACTS 1; MATTHEW 24; GENESIS 6)

True/False

1.   Those are killed all the day long by whom   T / F
     Christ's apostle were so.
     Romans 8:36 says, *As it is written, for their sake*
     we are killed all the day long; we are accounted as
     sheep for the slaughter.

     Look at this, they are all the day long in fear
     of being killed; sinking under that which lies
     upon them, and yet still trembling for fear of
     worse, and looking after those things which
     are coming upon the world.

2.   As people will do, the disciples asked   T / F
     concerning the times, when shall these things
     be? Christ gave them no answer to that, after
     what number of days and years his prediction
     should be accomplished, for it is not for us to
     know the time.

     Acts 1:7 says, *And he said unto them, it is not for*
     you to know the times or the seasons, which the
     Father has put in his own power.

3.   That question he answers fully, for we are   T / F
     concerned to understand the signs of the
     times, so Jesus says, **and in the morning, it**
     will be foul weather today: for the sky is
     red and lowing Oh you hypocrites, you can
     discern the face of the sky; but can you not
     discern the signs of the time?

4.   It is observable that what Christ said to his   T / F
disciples tends more to engage their caution
than to satisfy their curiosity; more to prepare
them for the events that should happen than
to give them a distinct idea of the events
themselves.

Matthew 24:35-36 says, *Jesus said* **heaven and
earth shall pass away, but my words shall
not pass away. But of that day and hour no
man, no, not the angels of heaven, but the
Father only.**

5.   Genesis 6:2-4 says, *The things that have been*   T / F
*shall be again. The world was full of violence and
it repented the Lord that he had made man on
the earth, and it grieved him at his heart. And he
said he would destroy man whom he had created
from the face of the earth; both man and beast and
every creeping thing, and the fowls of the air; for it
repented me that he has made them.*

CHAPTER 4: WORKSHEET 8
CONCERNING JESUS' PROPHECIES: THE LAST DAYS
(MARK 13; EXRA 6:14-15)

True/False

1. Ezra 6:14-15. About fifteen years before Jesus was born in (20 B. C.), Herod the Great began to remodel and rebuild the temple, which had stood for nearly 500 years since the days of Ezra. Ezra 6: 15 says, And this house was finished on the third day of the month.   T / F

2. Ezra 6:14 says, they built, and finished it, according to the _____of whose what of what _____

3. Mark 13 verse 1 _____, 3 _____ or 6_____ The disciples said unto the Master, see what manner of stones and what buildings are here.   T / F

4. Mark 13 verse _____ Jesus said see these great buildings there shall not be left one stone: upon another, that shall not be thrown down.   T / F

5. a. Evil spirits, or demons, are ruled by Satan.   T / F
    b. Book_____ chapter_____
    verse_____

6. a. Evil spirits work to tempt people to sin.   T / F
    b. Book_____ chapter_____
    verse_____

7. a. Evil spirits were created by Satan.   T / F
    b. Book_____ chapter_____
    verse_____

8. God the creator of all things. The demons, were fallen angels who joined Satan in his rebellion. b. Book_____ chapter_____ verse_____   T / F

9.   All disease comes from Satan.   T / F

10   Demons can cause a person to become mute,   T / F
        deaf, blind, or insane.

11.   In every case where demons confronted Jesus,   T / F
        they lost their power.

12.   God limits what evil spirits can do.   T / F

13.   They can do nothing without God's   T / F
        permission.

14.   During Jesus' life on earth, demons were   T / F
        allowed to be very active to demonstrate once
        and for all Christ's power and authority over
        them.

CHAPTER 4: WORKSHEET 9
CONCERNING JESUS' PROPHECIES: THE LAST DAYS
FALSE TEACHERS (MARK 13; MATTHEW 24)

<u>True/False</u>

1. a. It is possible for Christians to be deceived
   b. Book_____ chapter_____   T / F
   verse_____

2. Convincing will be the arguments and proofs   T / F
   from deceivers in the end times that it will be
   difficult not to fall away from Christ.

3. If we are prepared, Jesus says, we can remain   T / F
   faithful.

4. To penetrate the disguises of false teachers   T / F
   we can question whether their prediction
   comes true, or do they have to revise them to
   fit what's already happened.

5. Does any teacher utilize a small section of the   T / F
   Bible to the neglect the whole?

6. Do the teaching contradict what the Bible says   T / F
   about God?

7. Do the teachings promote hostility toward   T / F
   other Christians?

8. Mark 13 :23 says, *But you take heed: behold, I*   T / F
   have foretold you all things.

9.   Mark 13:22 says, *For false Christs and false   T / F
      prophets shall rise, and shall: show signs and
      wonders, to seduce, if it were possible, even the
      elect.*

10   Mark 13:22 says, *But you take heed. Behold, I have   T / F
      foretold you all things.* Mark chapter_____
      verse_____

11.   Although we do not know exactly what the   T / F
      temple looked like, but it must have been
      beautiful.

12.   Matthew 24:1 the disciples came to Jesus to   T / F
      show him the building of the temple

13.   Matthew 24 verse 7_____ 6_____ or 5_____   T / F
      says, for many shall come in my name, saying,
      I am Christ; and shall deceive many.

14.   Matthew 24:9 says, *Then shall they deliver you
      up to be afflicted, and shall kill you: and you shall
      be hated of all nations for my name's sake.*

CHAPTER 4: WORKSHEET 10
CONCERNING JESUS' PROPHECIES:
THE LAST DAYS
FALSE TEACHERS (MARK 13; MATTHEW 24)

<u>True/False</u>

1.   The false teachers were proud of their
      humility! This false humility brought attention   T / F
      and praise to themselves rather than to God.

2.   Colossians 2:18. Should you let any man
      beguile you of your reward in a voluntary
      humility and worshiping of angels, intruding
      into those things which had not seen, vainly
      puffed up by his fleshly mind.
      [Cross out the wrong words and write in the
      correct words]

3.   The false teachers were claiming that God was   T / F
      far away and could not be approached only
      through various levels of angels.

4.   The Bible teaches that angels are God's   T / F
      servants. God forbids worshiping them.

5.   Exodus 20:3-4 says, *You shall serve no other gods*   T / F
      before me. You shall not make unto you any graven
      image, or any likeness of anything that is in heaven
      above, or that is in the earth beneath, or that is in
      the water under the earth.

6.   Revelation 22:8-9, John said he saw these
      things, and heard them. *And when he heard and*
      seen, he fell down to worship before the feet of the
      angel which showed him these things. Was John
      wrong to do that? Yes / No
      WHY? _____

7.   *Then he said unto him, you see do not: for I am your*   T / F
      fellow servant, and of your brethren the prophets,
      and of them which keep the sayings of this book:
      worship God only. The expression "unspiritual
      mind" means that these people had a self-
      made religion.

8.   a. The false teaches were trying to deny the   T / F
      significance of the body by saying it was
      evil, but their desire for attention from others
      showed that, in reality, they were obsessed
      with the physical realm.
      b. Book_____   chapter_____
      verse____

9.   Colossians 2:9 says, *For in him dwell all the*   T / F
      fullness of the Godhead body.

CHAPTER 4: WORKSHEET 11
CONCERNING JESUS' PROPHECIES: THE LAST DAYS
CHRISTIANS FACE PERSECUTION

True/False

1. You may not be facing intense persecution now, but Christians in other parts of the world are, not only in other parts of the world but next door or in the same church. As you hear about Christians suffering because of their faith, remember that they are your brothers and sisters in Christ.   T / F

2. We are to pray for fellow Christians and ask God what we can do to help them in their troubles.   T / F

3. When one part suffers, the whole body suffers but when all the parts join together to ease the suffering, the whole body benefits.   T / F

4. I-Corinthians 12:26, *Tells us whether one member suffers, all the members suffer with it; or one member be honored, all the members rejoice with it.*   T / F

5. If you cut off one of your hands, the other hand suffers because of it. You have to learn how to do things with one hand, it will be hard and take some time in doing it.   T / F

6. 2-Kings 3:13. Old Testament frequently mentions false prophets.   T / F

7. 2-Kings 3:13. *Elisha said unto the king of Israel, what have I to do with you?*   T / F

8. Isaiah 44:25 says something about wise turning men backward and making their knowledge foolish.   T / F

9. Jeremiah 23:16 says, *Thus said the Lord of hosts, Hearken not unto the words of the prophets that prophesy unto you: they make you vain.*   T / F

10   Jeremiah 23:16 also says, *They speak a vision of*   T / F
their own heart.

11.   Ezekiel 13:2-3 says, *Son of man, prophesy against*   T / F
the prophets of Israel.

12.   Ezekiel 13 verse 3____ or 2____ The prophet   T / F
was to prophesy to, was he prophesying out
of his own heart.

13.   Ezekiel 13 verse ____God told him to say, *Woe*   T / F
unto the foolish prophets, that follow their own
spirit.

14.   Zech 13:2 says, *That it shall come to pass in that*   T / F
day, said the Lord of hosts, that I will cut off the
names: of the idols out of the land, and they shall
no more be remembered.

CHAPTER 5.
OBEYING THE
TEACHINGS OF JESUS

1. MESSIAH A RELIGIOUS TITLE

From a religious aspect, Messiah was a religious title. It could be translated into political terms as "king of the Jews." Anyone who claimed to be king of the Jews, as Jesus claimed presented a challenge to the Roman Emperor's rule in Judea. On the charge, the Roman governor Pilate finally convicted Jesus. This was the charge spelled out in the inscription fixed above His head on the cross. Death by crucifixion was the penalty for sedition by one who was not a Roman citizen.

2. DEATH AND BURIAL OF JESUS

Death Did Not End Jesus' Work. With the death and burial of Jesus, the narrative of His earthly career came to an end. With His resurrection on the third day He lives and works forever as the exalted Lord. His appearances to His disciple after His resurrection assured them that He was "alive after His suffering."

The Disciples Were Eyewitnesses. Luke says that the disciples were eye witnesses to all that had happened to Jesus Christ during His life before His crucifixion ("suffering"), and the 40 days after His resurrection as He taught them more about the kingdom of God.

People Still Doubt. Today there are still people who doubt Jesus' resurrection. Jesus appeared to the disciples on many occasions after His resurrection, proving that He was alive.

The Reappearance of Christ Strengthened Followers. Let us look at the change the resurrection made in the disciples' lives. At Jesus' death they scattered. One would think they were disillusioned and they feared for their lives. I can understand the disillusion they could have had. When you don't have Christ in your life you are at a loss. After seeing the resurrected Christ they were fearless and risked everything to spread the Good News about Him around the world. They faced imprisonment, beatings, rejection, and martyrdom, yet they never compromised their mission.

3. SPREADING THE GOOD NEWS

<u>Enthusiasm Swept the Early Church</u>. The men would not have risked their lives for something they knew was a fraud. They knew Jesus was raised from the dead, and the early church was fired with their enthusiasm to tell others. It is important to know this so we can have confidence in our testimony concerning the new birth we have the witness of Christ in us as having a new life in him. Twenty centuries later we can have that same confidence that our faith is based on fact.

<u>Spread the Good News</u>. When He returned to heaven, God's kingdom would remain in the hearts of all believers through the presence of the Holy Spirit. The kingdom of God will not be fully realized until Jesus Christ comes again to judge all people and remove all evil from the world. Before that time, believers are to work to spread God's kingdom across the world which is the Good News. The book of Acts records how this work was begun. What the early church started, we must continue.

To whom also He showed himself alive after His passion by many infallible proofs, being seen of them forty days, and speaking of the things pertaining to the Kingdom of God (Acts 1:3).

<u>Jesus Taught Distinctive Spiritual Truths</u>. These appearances also enabled them to make the transition in their experience from the form in which they had known Him earlier to the new way in which they would be related to Him by the Holy Spirit. Just as His life was unique, so were His teachings known for their fresh and new approach. Jesus taught several distinctive spiritual truths that set Him apart from any other religious leader who ever lived.

4. COMMITMENT TO GOD

<u>Jesus Complied With God's Will</u>. While praying, Jesus was aware of what doing the Father's will would cost him. He understood the suffering He was about to encounter, and He did not want to have to endure the horrible experience. But He prayed, *Not what I will, but what your will.* Anything worth having costs something. Here's a question to you concerning your commitment to God: What does it cost you? Are you willing to pay the price to gain something worthwhile in the end?

And He said, Abba, Father, all things are possible unto you, take away this cup from me: nevertheless not what I will, but what your will (Mark 14:36).

<u>Our Father</u>. The term of affection that children use when they address their father at home or spoke about him to others. It was not unusual for God to be addressed in prayer as "my Father" or "our Father." It was most unusual for Him to be called Abba Father. By using this term, Jesus expressed His sense of nearness to God and His total trust in him. In doing so He taught His followers to look to God with the trust that children show when they expect their earthly father to provide them with food, clothes, and shelter.

<u>The Lord's Prayer: Jesus Taught the Disciples How to Pray</u>. This attitude is especially expressed in the Lord's Prayer, which may be regarded as a brief summary of Jesus' teaching. In this prayer the disciples were taught to pray for the fulfillment of God's eternal purpose, the coming of His kingdom and to ask Him for daily bread, forgiveness of sin, and deliverance from temptation.

5. PROCLAMATION OF THE GOOD NEWS

<u>Jesus Healed the Sick and Proclaimed the Kingdom of God.</u> In Jesus' healing of the sick and proclamation of good news to the poor, the kingdom of God was visibly present but it was not yet fully realized. Otherwise, it would not have been necessary for Him to tell His disciples to pray, *Your kingdom come.* We mustn't look at this as not being Israel's freedom from Rome. The phrase *Your*

kingdom come is a reference to God's spiritual reign: *Thy kingdom come, thy will be done in earth, as it is in heaven*, God's kingdom was announced in the covenant with Abraham.

And I say unto you, that many shall come from the east and west, and shall sit down with Abraham and Isaac, and Jacob in the kingdom of heaven (Matthew 8:11).

There shall be weeping and gnashing of teeth. When you shall see Abraham and Isaac and Jacob, and all the prophets, in the kingdom of God, and You yourselves thrust out. As believers in their hearts being present in Christ's reign, according to Luke and Revelation, (Luke 13:28)

Neither shall they say, Lo here! Or, Lo there! For, behold, the kingdom of God is within you (Luke 17:21)

And I saw heaven and a new earth: for the first heaven and the first earth were passed away and there was no more sea (Revelation 21:1).

God's Will be Done. According to Matthew 6:10, when we pray *your will be done,* we are not resigning ourselves to fate, but praying that God's perfect purpose will be accomplished in this world as well as in the next, which will be in the new heaven as in earth.

6. THE NEW KINGDOM OF JESUS WILL COME WITH POWER

Disciples Would See the Kingdom of God. One day Jesus taught that the kingdom will come with power and some of them would live to see that day. There are several meanings to what Jesus meant when He said, *Some of the disciples would see the kingdom of God come with power*:

- It could have been foretelling of His transfiguration,

- His resurrection and ascension,

- The coming of the Holy Spirit at the day of Pentecost, or

- His second coming.

The transfiguration is a strong possibility, because Mark immediately tells that story. In the transfiguration (Mark 9:2-8), Peter, James and John saw Jesus' glory, identity, and the power as the Son of God (2-Peter 1:16).

He said unto them, Verily I say unto you, that there be some of them that stand here, which shall not taste of death, till they have seen the kingdom of God come with power (Mark 9:1).

Jesus Gave the Example of Honor and Service. In the kingdom of God the way to honor is the way of service. In this respect, Jesus set a worthy example, choosing to give service instead of receiving it.

7. THE MESSAGE AND LAW JESUS TAUGHT

The Way of the Kingdom. The ethical teaching of Jesus was part of His proclamation of the kingdom of God. Only by His death and resurrection could the divine rule be established. Even while the kingdom of God was in the process of inauguration during His ministry, its principles could be translated into action in the lives of His followers.

The Sermon on the Mount. The most familiar presentation of these principles is found in the Sermon on the Mount recorded in Matthew chapters 5-7 addressed to His disciples. These principles showed how those who were already children of the kingdom ought to live.

The Law of Moses. The people who Jesus taught already had a large body of ethical teaching in the Old Testament law but a further body or oral interpretation and application had grown up around the law of Moses over the centuries. Jesus declared that He had come to fulfill the law, not to destroy it.

Think not that I am come to destroy the law or the prophets: I am not come to destroy, but to fulfill (Matthew 5:17).

The Two Greatest Commandments. He emphasized its ethical quality by summarizing it in terms of what He called the two great commandments: *You shall love your God* (Deuteronomy 6:5) *and you shall love the Lord your God with all your heart, and with all your soul, and with all your might.*

You shall not avenge, nor bear any grudge against the children of your people, but you shall love your neighbor as yourself: I am the Lord (Leviticus 19:18).

On these two commandments, He said, *Hang all the law and the prophets* (Matthew 22:40).

Jesus Did not Come to Destroy the Law. In Matthew 5:17, Jesus was talking about God's moral and ceremonial law. This means to characterize and form Israel's heart and minds to love God with all their hearts and minds. Israel's history was that these laws had been often misquoted and misapplied. Religious leaders had turned the law into a confusing mass of rules. In studying we can see why church people are in such a mass in their minds.

Jesus Spoke Against the Abuses of the Law. When Jesus talked about a new way to understand God's law, He was actually trying to bring people back to its original purpose. Jesus did not speak against the law itself, but against the abuses and excesses to which it had been subjected.

For the Law was given through Moses; grace and truth were realized through Jesus Christ (John 1:17).

The Pharisees Rated the Laws in Importance. The Pharisees had classified over 600 laws and often tried to distinguish the more important from the less important. So one of them who was an expert in the law asked Jesus to identify the most important law. Jesus quoted from Deuteronomy 6:5.

Obey God's Commandments. Jesus was not showing that He was claiming uniqueness or originality for His ethical teaching. One of Jesus' purposes was to explain the ancient law of God. By fulfilling these two commands, a person keeps all the others. They summarize the Ten Commandments and the other Old Testament moral law. A lot of people don't really look at the moral law; they just look at the fact that Jesus came and gave these two because it fulfilled the Old Testament law. Jesus says if we truly love God and our neighbor, we will naturally keep the commandments. This is looking at God's law positively. Rather than worrying about all we should not do, we should concentrate on all we can do to show our love for God and others. There was a distinctiveness and freshness about His teaching, as He declared His authority.

But I say to you, you have heard that it was said by them of old time, you shall not kill; and whosoever shall kill shall be in danger of the judgment. But I say unto you, that whosoever is angry with His brother without cause shall be in danger of the judgment; and whosoever shall say to His brother, Rica, shall be in danger of the council; but whosoever shall say, you fool, shall be in danger of hell fire (Matthew 5:21-22).

Be willing to be committed to listening to His words and doing them while building a secure foundation for your life.

8. PRACTICE OBEDIENCE

To build "on the rock" means to be a hearing person, responding not as a phony, superficial one. Practicing obedience becomes the solid foundation to weather the storms of life (James 1:22-27).

[22] But be doers of the word, and not hearers only, deceiving your own selves, [23] For if any be a hearer of the word, and not a doer, He is like unto a man beholding His natural face in a glass: [24] for He behold himself, and go His way, and straightaway forget what manner of man He was; [25] but whoso look into the perfect law of liberty, and continue therein, He being not a forgetful hearer, but a doer of the work, this man shall be blessed in His deed. [26] If any man among you seems to be religious, and bridle not His tongue, but deceived His own heart, this man's religion is vain. [27] Pure religion and undefiled before God and the Father is this, to visit the fatherless and widows in their affliction, and to keep Himself unspotted from the world (James 1:22-27).

Build a Strong Foundation of God's Word. Also read Luke 6:46-49. Disobeying is like having crises in your life. Obeying God is like building a house on a strong, solid foundation that stands firm when storms come. When life has no calm and the world seems to fall around us and our foundations don't seem to matter, and crises come, our foundation is again tested. Be sure your life is built on the solid foundation of knowing and trusting in Jesus Christ. Being obedient and repentant according to the word of God through Jesus Christ will give you that strong foundation you will need in time of storms.

But He that hears and does not is like a man who without a foundation built a house upon the earth against which the stream did beat vehemently, and immediately it fell; and the ruin of that house was great (Luke 6:49).

9. JESUS SETTLED THE QUESTION OF DIVORCE

In Our Image. Why does God use the plural form, *Let us make man in our image?*

- One view is through references to the (Trinity,) (God the Father,) (Jesus Christ His Son), and the (Holy Spirit,) all of whom are God.

- Another view is that the plural wording is used to denote (majesty) (Kings) traditionally use the plural form in speaking of themselves.

The spirit of God has made me, and the breath of the Almighty have given me life (Job 33:4).

You sent me forth your spirit, they are created: and you renew the face of the earth (Psalms 104:30).

- The another view is being known in saying we know that God's Spirit was present in the creation.

For by Him were all things created, that are in heaven, and that are in earth, visible and invisible, whether they be thrones, or "dominions, or principalities, or powers: all things were created by him, and for him (Colossians 1:16).

- We know that according to the written word that Christ, God's Son was at work in the creation.

And God said, let us make man in our image, after our likeness: and let them have dominion over the fish of the sea, and over the fowl of the air, and over the cattle, and over all the earth and every creeping thing that creep upon the earth. So God created man in His own image, in the image of God created He him, male and female created He them. God made both man and woman in His image (Genesis 1:26-27).

God Made Both Man and Woman in His Image. Neither man nor woman is made more in the image of God than the other. From the beginning the Bible places both man and woman at the pinnacle of God's creation. Neither sex is exalted, and neither is depreciated.

The Marriage of Adam and Eve Was a Gift. They were created perfect for each other. Marriage was not just for convenience as some seem to think and take it, nor was it brought about by any culture.

They were both naked, the man and His wife, and were not ashamed (Genesis 2:24-25).

Divorce Was an Attempt to Undo the Work of God. Since husband and wife were made one by the creator's decree, Jesus pointed out that divorce was an attempt to undo the work of God. If the law later allowed for divorce in certain situations, that was a concession to men's inability to keep the commandment. It was not so in the beginning, Jesus declared, and it should not be so for those who belong to the kingdom of God.

Old Testament Law for Divorce. Looking more into the Old Testament law gives more understanding concerning a divorce. Some think this passage of the O.T. supports divorce. That is not the case. It simply recognizes a practice that already existed in Israel. All four of these verses must be read to understand the point of the passage. It certainly is not suggesting that a man should divorce His wife on a whim. Divorce was a permanent and final act for the couple. Once the divorce was permanent and the couple were remarried to others, they could never be remarried to each. This restriction was to prevent casual remarriage after a frivolous separation. The intention was to make people think twice before divorcing.

[1] When a man has taken a wife, and married her, and it come to pass that she finds no favor in his eyes, because he has found some uncleanness in her, then let him write her a bill of divorcement, and give it in her hand, and send her out of his house. [2] And when she is departed out of his house, she may go and be another man's wife. [3] And if the latter husband hate her, and write her a bill of divorcement, and give it in her hand, and send her out of his house, or if the later husband die, which took her to be his wife; [4] Her former husband, which sent her away, may not take her again to be his wife, after that she is defiled; for that is abomination before the Lord your God given you for (inheritance) (Deuteronomy 24:1-4).

This last verse is the part everyone seems to left out, (the inheritance which is what God has given you from the beginning of time, Adam and Eve were to forever to be together).

<u>Committing Adultery</u>. The Old Testament law said it is wrong for a person to have sex with someone other than their own spouse.

You shall not commit adultery (Exodus 20: 14).

But Jesus said that the desire to have sexual intimacy with someone other than your spouse is mental adultery and that is sin. Jesus emphasized that if the act is wrong then so is the intention to be faithful to your spouse with your body and yet not with your mind. Having the intent will break the trust in the marriage. Jesus is not condemning natural interest in the opposite sex or even healthy sexual desire, but the deliberate and repeated filling of one's mind with fantasies that would be evil if acted out.

You have heard that it was said by them of old time, you shall not commit adultery. But I say unto you, that whosoever looks on a woman to lust after her has committed adultery with her already in his heart (Matthew 5:27-28).

10. GENEROUSITY IN GIVING (LUKE 6:29-30)

<u>Jesus Addressed Laws About Property</u>. Jesus' attitude and teaching also made many laws about property irrelevant for His followers. They should be known as people who give, not as people who get. *If someone demands your cloak* which is your (outer garment), *Jesus said give it to him, and give your (undergarment) as well.* There is more to life than abundance of possession; in fact, He pointed out, material wealth can be a hindrance to one's spiritual life.

<u>Jesus Addressed Laws About Material Wealth</u>. Jesus also says that the good life has nothing to do with being wealthy, so be on guard against greed and desire for what we don't have. This is the exact opposite of what society usually says.

He said unto them, take heed, and beware of covetousness: for a man's life consists not in the abundance of the things which he possesses (Luke 12:15).

Advertisers spend millions of dollars to entice us to think if we buy more and more of their products, we will be happier, more fulfilled, more comfortable. How do you respond to the constant pressure to buy? Learn to tune out expensive enticements and concentrate instead in the truly good life living in a relationship with God and doing His work. The wise man, therefore, will get rid of it because *it is easier for a camel to go through the eye of a needle than for a rich man to enter the kingdom of God* (Luke 10:25).

Those who would be saved must apply themselves to Christ and His teachings, and enquire of him. It is peculiar to the Christian religion both to show eternal life, and to show the way to it. It is good design to be taught. With a bad design, to pick quarrels with him; He tempted him, saying Master, what shall I do? It is not so much the good words as the good intention of them that Christ looks at.

11. BLESSINGS AND GOODWILL

<u>Ethical Behavior of Followers</u>. Jesus insisted that more is expected of His followers than the ordinary morality of decent people. Their ethical behavior should *exceed the righteousness of the scribes and Pharisees* (Matthew 2:20).

For I say unto you, that except your righteousness exceed the righteousness of the scribes and Pharisees, you shall in no wise enter into the kingdom of heaven (Matthew 2:20).

If you love (only) those who love you, He asked, What credit is that to you? For even sinners love who love them (Luke 6:32).

The higher standard of the kingdom of God called for acts of love to enemies and words of blessing and goodwill to persecutors. The children of the kingdom should not insist on their legal rights but cheerfully give them up in response to the supreme law of love. If Jesus did not come to abolish the law, does that mean all the Old Testament laws still apply to us today? In the Old Testament, there were three categories of law:

- ceremonial law,

- civil law, and

- moral law.

<u>Ceremonial Law</u>. Ceremonial law relates specifically to Israel's worship (Leviticus 1:2-3). For example, its primary purpose was to point forward to Jesus Christ. These laws were no longer necessary after Jesus' death and resurrection.

Speak unto the children of Israel and say unto them, if any man of you brings an offering unto the Lord, you shall bring your offering of the cattle, even of the head and of the flock. If his offering be a bunt sacrifice of the head let him offer a male without blemish: He shall offer it of his own voluntary will at the door of the tabernacle of the congregation before the Lord (Leviticus 1:2-3).

While we are no longer bound by the ceremonial law because the principles behind them to worship and love a holy God still apply. Jesus was often accused by the Pharisees of violating the ceremonial law.

The Civil Law. The civil law applied to daily living in Israel (Deuteronomy 24:10-11), because modern society and culture are so radically different from that time and setting. All of those guidelines cannot be followed specifically. However, the principles behind the commands are timeless and should guide our conduct. Jesus demonstrated these principles by leaving examples for us to go by in our daily lives today.

The Moral Law. The moral law such as the Ten Commandments is the direct command of God, and it requires strict obedience (Exodus 20:13). The moral law reveals the nature and will of God, and it still applies today. Jesus obeyed the moral law completely. This is why I said He left us examples to live by today, so those principles apply today to us.

Love and Obedience. Jesus was saying we need a different kind of righteousness altogether, which is love and obedience. If we don't love, how can we be obedient to God and our fellow man and not just having a more intense version of the Pharisees' legal righteous compliance. Our righteousness must come from what God does in us, not what we can do by ourselves. It must be God-centered not self-centered. It must be based on reverence for God, not approval from people, and go beyond keeping the law to living by the principles behind the law.

12. PRINCIPALS TO NONVIOLENCE

The Principles of Nonviolence. The principle of nonviolence is deeply ingrained in Jesus' teachings. In His references to the "men of violence" who tried to bring in the kingdom of God by force, Jesus gave no sign that He approved of their ideals or methods. The course which He called for was the way of peace and submission. He urged us not to strike back against unjust acts or oppression but to turn the other cheek, to go a second mile when our service was demanded for one mile, and to take the inactive in returning good for evil.

<u>Nonviolence Did Not Appeal to the People</u>. The way of nonviolence did not appeal to the people. The crowd chose the militant Barabbas when they were given the opportunity to have either Jesus or Barabbas set free. But the attitude expressed in the shout, *Not this man, but Barabbas!* was the spirit that would one day level Jerusalem and bring misery and suffering to the Jewish nation.

<u>Rebellion Against Roman Rule</u>. Barabbas had taken part in a rebellion against the Roman government. Although an enemy of Rome, He was a hero to some of the Jews. Ironically, Barabbas was guilty of the crime for which Jesus was accused. Barabbas means "son of the father," which was actually Jesus' position with God.

And there was one name Barabbas, which lay bound with them that had made insurrection with him, who had committed murder in the insurrection (Mark 15:7).

Now at that feast the governor was wont to release unto the people a prisoner, whom they would. And they had then a notable prisoner, called Barabbas (Matthew 27:16-17).

13. JESUS TEACHES THE SUPREME EXAMPLE

<u>The Supreme Example is God</u>. The supreme example in the teaching of Jesus and the highest of all incentives is the example of God. This was no principle. The central section of Leviticus is called "the law of holiness" because of its recurring theme: *I am the Lord your God; be holy, for I am holy* (Leviticus 11 :44). This bears a close resemblance to Jesus' words in Luke 6:36, ***Be merciful, just as your Father also is merciful***. The children of God should imitate their Father's character.

<u>Show Kindness to All</u>. He does not discriminate between the good and the evil in bestowing rain and sunshine; likewise, His followers should not discriminate in showing kindness to all. He

delights in forgiving sinners; His children should also be marked by a forgiving spirit.

The Key to Leviticus Law. These verses provide a key to understanding all the laws and regulations in Leviticus. God wanted His people to be holy and set apart, different, and unique, just as He is holy. He knew they had two options:

- to be separate and holy, or

- to compromise with their pagan neighbors and become corrupt.

This is why He called them out of idolatrous Egypt and set them apart as a unique nation, dedicated to worshiping Him alone and living moral lives. That is also why He designed laws and restrictions to help them remain separate both socially and spiritually from a wicked pagan nation they would encounter in Canaan.

For I am the Lord your God: you shall therefore sanctify yourselves, and you shall be holy, for I am holy; neither shall you defile yourselves with any manner of creeping things that creep upon the earth. For I am the Lord that bring you up out of the land of Egypt, to be your God, you shall therefore be holy, for I am holy (Leviticus 11:44-45).

Remain Separate from the Word's Wickedness. Christians today also are called to be holy.

But as He who has called you are holy, so you are holy in all manner of conversation (1-Peter 1:15).

Like the Israelites, we should remain spiritually separate from the world's wickedness. We rub shoulders with unbelievers every day. But God doesn't ask us to accomplish this on our own. Through the death of His Son, He will *present us who have lived righteous before Him and have stayed separate from the wicked. In the body of His flesh through death, to present us holy and unbelievable and unreprovable in His sight* (Colossians 1:22).

14. JESUS WAS GOD'S EXAMPLE

The Example of the Heavenly Father was Shown Through Jesus. The example of the heavenly Father shown through the Son here on earth is one and the same because Jesus came to reveal the Father. Jesus' life was the practical demonstration of His ethical teaching. To His disciples He declared, *I have given you an example, that you should do as I have done to you* (John 13:1-17).

For I have given you an example, that you should do as I have done (John 13:1-17).

Jesus was the Model Servant. He showed His servant attitude to His disciples. Washing guests' feet was a job for a household servant to carry out when guests arrived. But Jesus wrapped a towel around His waist as the lowliest slave would do, and washed and dried His disciples' feet. If even God in the flesh is willing to serve us, as His followers we must also be servants, willing to serve in any way that glorifies God. The question is: Are you willing to follow Christ's example of serving? There is a special blessing for those who not only agree that humble service is Christ's way, but who also follow through and do it.

If you know these things, happy are you if you do them (John 13:17).

Jesus Washed the Feet of the Disciples. Imagine Peter watching Jesus washing the others' feet and moving closer to him. Seeing his Master behave like a slave must have confused Peter. This is the world's way of looking at things. Seeing it in a person who is doing the right thing is showing love for others. Peter still did not understand Jesus' teaching as a leader. A person must be a servant to be able to lead. This is not a comfortable passage for leaders who find it hard to serve those beneath them. How do you treat those who work under you (whether they are children, employees, or volunteers)?

Jesus Taught by Example. Jesus did not wash His disciples' feet just to get them to be nice to each other. His far greater goal was to extend His mission on earth after He was gone. These men were to move into the world serving God, serving each other, and serving all people to whom they took the message of salvation.

<u>Jesus Exceeded Expectations</u>.

- A man was expecting to be healed: Jesus also forgave his sins (Mark 2:1-12)

- The disciples were expecting a day of fishing: They found the savior (Luke 5:1-11)

<u>The Pharisees were Asking for Miraculous Signs.</u> They were not sincerely seeking to know Jesus. Jesus knew they had already seen enough miraculous proof to convince them that He was the Messiah if they would just open their hearts. It seems that they had already decided not to believe in him, and more miracles would not change that.

Then certain of the scribes and of the Pharisees answered, saying Master, we would see a sign from you (Matthew 12:38).

Many people have said, "If I could just see a real miracle, then I could really believe in God." Jesus response to the Pharisees applies to us. We have plenty of evidence in Jesus' birth, death, resurrection, and ascension, and centuries of His work in believers around the world. Instead of looking for additional evidence or miracles, accept what God has already given. He may use your life as evidence to reach another person.

15. HONORING A KING

<u>Matthew (Levi) the Tax Collector</u>. Matthew (Levi) was a Jewish tax collector who became one of Jesus' disciples. The Gospel forms the concerning link between the Old and New Testament because of its emphasis on the fulfillment of prophecy. He wrote in A.D. 60-65.

Do not think that I have come to abolish the Law or the Prophets; I have not come to abolish them but to fulfill them (Matthew 5:17).

- <u>Purpose</u>: To prove that Jesus is the Messiah, the eternal King

- <u>Key People</u>: Jesus, Mary, Joseph, John the Baptist, the disciples, the religious, Caiaphas, Pilate, Mary Magdalene

- <u>Key Places</u>: Bethlehem, Jerusalem, Capernaum, Galilee, Judea

- Matthew is filled with Messianic language ("Son of David'" is used throughout) and Old Testament references (53 quotes and 76 other references).

This Gospel was not written as a chronological account, its purpose was to present the clear evidence that Jesus is the messiah, the Savior.

<u>Protocol for Honoring a King</u>. As the motorcade slowly winds through the city, thousands pack the sidewalks hoping to catch a glimpse. Marching bands with great fanfare announce the arrival of a head of state, and protective agents scan the crowd and run alongside the limousine. These are the protocols and modem symbols of position and evidences of importance heralding the arrival of a head of state. Whether they are leaders by birth or election, we honor and respect them. This is my Jesus Christ, He is all of this to me, He died for me, He did all of that for me to give me access to eternal life.

<u>The Prophecies Announcing the Messiah Overlooked</u>. The Jews waited for a leader who had been promised centuries before by prophets. They believed that this leader, who was the Messiah (the "anointed) one of God would rescue them from their Roman oppressors and establish a new kingdom. As their King, He would rule the world with justice. Many Jews overlooked prophecies that also spoke of the Messiah as a suffering servant who would be rejected and killed. It is no wonder that few recognized Jesus as the Messiah. How could this humble carpenter's son from Nazareth be their king? But Jesus was and is the King of all the earth.

<u>Matthew (Levi) was one of the Disciples</u>. Matthew (Levi) was one of Jesus' 12 disciples. Once he was a despised tax collector, but his

life was changed by this man from Galilee. Matthew wrote this Gospel to his fellow Jews to prove that Jesus is the Messiah and to explain God's kingdom.

Matthew's Genealogy of Jesus. Matthew begins His account by giving Jesus' genealogy. He then tells of Jesus' birth and early years, including the family's escape to Egypt from the murderous Herod and their return to Nazareth. Following Jesus' baptism by John (Matthew 3:17) and His defeat of Satan in the desert, Jesus began His public ministry by calling His first disciple and giving the Sermon on the Mount (Matthew 5:7). Matthew shows Christ's authority by reporting His miracles of healing the sick and the demon possessed, and even raising the dead.

And Lo a voice from heaven, saying, this is My beloved Son in whom I am well pleased (Matthew 3: 17).

16. THE SIGNIFICANCE OF JESUS

Jesus Continued to Teach. Despite of opposition from the Pharisees and others in the religious establishment (Matthew 12-15), Jesus continued to teach concerning the kingdom of heaven (Matthew 16-20). During this time, Jesus spoke with His disciples about His imminent death and resurrection (Matthew 16:21), and revealed His true identity to Peter, James, and John (Matthew 21:1-11). Soon opposition mounted and Jesus knew the future and what they could expect before His return (Matthew 24) and how to live until then (Matthew 25).

Jesus' Final Days. Matthew 26-28 focuses on Jesus' final days on earth: the Last Supper, His prayer in Gethsemane, the betrayal by Judas, the flight of the disciples, Peter's denial, the trials before Caiaphas and Pilate, Jesus' final words on the cross, and His burial in a borrowed tomb. The story does not end there, for the Messiah rose from the dead-- conquering death-- and then told His followers to continue His work by making disciples in all nations.

Matthew's Message. As you read this Gospel, listen to Matthew's clear message concerning the Jesus Christ, the King of kings and

Lord of Lords. Celebrate His victory over evil and death and make Jesus the Lord of your life.

Rejected by the Jews. Jesus was formally presented to the nation of Israel, but rejected by them. How strange for the king to be accused, arrested, and crucified. Jesus demonstrated His power even over death through His resurrection, and gained access for us into His kingdom. With all this evidence that Jesus is God's Son we, too, should accept Him as our lord.

(1) Jesus begins His ministry
(2) Jesus gives the Sermon on the Mount
(3) Jesus performs many miracles
(4) Jesus teaches about the kingdom
(5) Jesus encounters differing reactions to His ministry
(6) Jesus faces conflict with the religious leaders
(7) Jesus teaches on the Mount of Olives

Jesus is Revealed as King of Kings. His miraculous birth, His life and teachings, His miracles, and His triumph over death show His true identity.

- Jesus cannot be equated with any person or power. He is the supreme ruler of time and eternal, heaven and earth, humans and angels.

- We should, give His rightful place as king of our lives.

Jesus was the Messiah. As the Messiah, Jesus was the one for whom the Jews had waited to deliver them from Roman oppression. Yet tragically, they didn't recognize Him when He came because His kingship was not what they expected. The true purpose of God's anointed deliverer was to die for the people to free them from sin's oppression.

- Because Jesus was sent by God, we can trust Him with our lives. It is worth everything we have to acknowledge Him and give ourselves to him, because He came to be our messiah, our Savior.

- The way to enter God's kingdom is by faith, believing in Christ to save us from sin and change our lives. We must do the work of His kingdom now to be prepared for His return.

Jesus Taught God's Message. Jesus taught people through sermons, illustrations, and parables. Through His teachings, He showed the true ingredient of faith and how to guard against a fruitless and hypocritical life.

- Jesus' teachings show us how to prepare for life in His eternal kingdom by living properly right now. He lived what He taught.

- We too must practice the example Jesus gave us.

The Resurrection. When Jesus rose from the dead, He rose in power as the true king. In His victory over death He established His credentials as king and His power and authority over evil.

- The resurrection shows Jesus' all powerful life for us. Not even death could stop His plan of offering eternal life.

- Those who believe in Jesus can hope for a resurrection like his. Our role is to tell His story to all the earth so that everyone may share in His victory.

Time Line

37 B.C.	Herod the Great begins rule
6/5 B.C.	Jesus is born
5/4 B.C.	Escape to Egypt
4/3 B.C.	Herod the Great dies
4/3 B.C.	Return to Nazareth
6 A.D.	Judea become a Roman province
6/7 A.D.	Jesus visits temple as a boy
14 A.D.	Tiberius Caesar because emperor
26 A.D.	Pontius Pilate appointed governor

25/27 A.D.	Jesus begins His ministry
29 A.D.	Jesus feeds 5,000
30 A.D.	Jesus is crucified, rises again, and ascends
	250 events in the life of Christ / A Harmony of the Gospels
	The Parables of Jesus' Miracles
	Comparison of the four Gospels
	Messianic Prophecies and fulfillments

17. PAUL'S MESSAGE WAS TO IMITATE JESUS

This theme of the imitation of Christ pervades the New Testament letter. It is especially evident in the writings of Paul, who was not personally acquainted with Jesus before he met Jesus on the Damascus Road.

Paul instructed His converts to follow "the meekness and gentleness of Christ" Paul's opponents questioned His authority. From 2-Corinthians 7:8-16 we know that the majority of Corinthian believers sided with Paul. Even so, a minority continued to slander him, saying that he was bold in his letters but had no authority in person. There didn't seem to be any response to this charge.

Read 2-Corinthians 7:8-16 also 2-Corinthians 10-13.

Now I Paul I beseech you by the meekness and gentleness of Christ, who in presence is base among you, but being absent, is bold toward you (2-Corinthians 10:1).

He also encouraged them to imitate him in the same manner that he imitated Christ. When Paul recommended to them the practice of all the Christian graces, he declared, *Put on the Lord Jesus Christ*, Paul said, *You are followers of me even as I also am of Christ* (1-Corinthian 11:1).

<u>Follow My Example</u>. After reading and studying the Scripture it is natural to ask, Why did Paul say, "Follow my example?" Paul wasn't being arrogant. He did not think of himself as sinless. At this time, the Corinthian believers did not know much about the life and ministry of Christ, the Gospels had not yet been written, and they did not know what Jesus was like. The best way to show these new Christians to Christ was to point them to a Christian who they trusted. Look at some of Paul's writings. He wrote, *Brethren, I beseech you, be as I am; for I am as you are; you have not injured me at all* (Galatians 4:12). Philip 3:17says, *Brethren, be followers together of me, and mark them which walk so as you have us for an example.*

<u>Words of Encouragement</u>.

Brethren, be followers together of me, and mark them which walk so as you have us for an example (Philip 3:17).

And you became followers of us, and of the Lord, having received the word in much affliction, with joy of the Holy Ghost (1-Thessalonians 1:6).

For you, brethren, became followers of the churches of God which in Judaea are in Christ Jesus: for you also have suffered like things of your own countrymen, even as they have of the Jews (1-Thessalonians 2: 14).

For yourselves know how you ought to follow us: for we behaved not ourselves disorderly among you (2-Thessalonians 3:7).

Not because we have not power, but to make ourselves an example unto you to follow us (2- Thessalonians 3:9).

CHAPTER 6. THE TITLES OF CHRIST

<u>The Doctrine of the Person of Christ</u>. The doctrine of the person of Christ, or Christology is one of the most important concerns of Christian Theology. The various aspects of the person of Christ are best seen by reviewing the titles that are applied to Him in the Bible.

1. SON OF MAN

<u>Jesus Referred to Himself as "the Son of Man</u>." According to the Scripture, the title "Son of Man" was Jesus' favorite way of referring to himself. He may have done this because it was not a commonly recognized title. It didn't have to be a recognized title already known by the people and associated with popular ideas. It means essentially "the man." I don't believe they used words like "He's the man" as we do today. Jesus is the only one who loved us enough to die for the sins of the world so His use of the title "Son of Man" took on new significance.

<u>Meanings of the Title "Son of Man"</u>. Jesus applied this title to himself in three distinct ways:

- Jesus used the title "Son of Man" in a general way as a substitute for "I."

- The title "Son of Man" emphasized that "the son of man must suffer."

- The title refers to the representative man as an agent of God.

- Jesus used the title to refer to himself as the one with authority delegated by God.

(1) <u>Jesus Used the Title "Son of Man" as a Substitute for the Pronoun "I."</u> A good example of this usage occurred when He contrasted John the Baptist, who "came neither eating bread nor drinking wine," with the "son of man, who has come eating and drinking."

<u>The Pharisees Justified Their Actions</u>. The Pharisees didn't seem to be troubled by their inconsistency toward John the Baptist and Jesus. The Pharisees were good at justifying their "'wisdom." Most of us can find compelling reasons to do or believe whatever suits our purposes. If we do not examine our ideas in the light of God's truth, we may be just as obviously self-serving as the Pharisees.

For John the Baptist came neither eating bread nor drinking wine and you say, he had a devil (Luke 7:33-34).

(2) <u>The Son of Man Must Suffer</u>.

- Jesus used the title for Himself to emphasize that "the son of man must suffer." The term implies that His suffering was foretold by the prophets.

- "The Son of Man" was Jesus' most common title for himself. It comes from Daniel's writings where the Son of Man is a heavenly figure who, in the end times, has authority and power.

I saw in the night visions and, behold, one like the Son of man came with the clouds of heaven, and came to the ancient of days, and they brought Him before him (Daniel 7:13).

<u>The Representative Man</u>. The name refers to Jesus as the Messiah, the representative man, the human agent of God who is vindicated by God. "Son of Man" is like Peter's confession of Jesus as the Christ and confirms its Messianic significance. Jesus spoke plainly and directly to His disciples about His death and resurrection. He began to prepare them for what was going to happen to Him by telling them three times that He would soon die.

And He began to teach them that the Son of man must suffer many things and be rejected of the elders, and of the chief priests, and scribes, and be killed, and after three days rise again (Mark 8:31).

For He taught His disciples, and said unto them, **The Son of man is delivered into the hands of men and they shall kill him; and after that He is killed, He shall rise the third day** (Mark 9:31).

Behold, we go up to Jerusalem, and the Son of man shall be delivered unto the chief priests, and unto the scribes, and they shall condemn Him to death, and shall deliver Him to the Gentiles. And they shall mock him, and shall scourge him, and shall spit upon him, and shall kill him, and the third day He shall rise again (Mark 10:33-34).

God's Plan Differed from the World's Expectations. In Mark 9:12-13 we can see that it was difficult for the disciples to grasp the idea that their Messiah would have to suffer. The Jews who studied the Old Testament prophecies expected the Messiah to be a great king like David, who would overthrow the enemy, which was the oppressive Roman rule. Their vision was limited to their own time and experience. They could not understand that the values of God's eternal kingdom were different from the values of the world. They wanted relief from their present problems, but the deliverance from sin is far more important than deliverance from physical suffering. The body does not like pain, so looking at it from that point I am sure we can understand where the people were coming from. They wanted relief from the physical suffering and the political oppression. This is why it was difficult for them to understand and accept Jesus. Our understanding of and appreciation for Jesus must go beyond what He can do for us here and now.

And He said to them, **Elijah does first come and restore all things. And yet how is it written of the Son of Man that He should suffer many things and be treated with contempt?** (Mark 9:12).

Jesus Referred to Elijah. When Jesus said that Elijah had indeed come, Jesus was speaking of John the Baptist who had fulfilled the role prophesied for Elijah.

And Jesus answered and said unto them, **Elias truly first came and restored all things. But I say unto you, that Elias has come already, and they knew Him not, but have done unto Him whatsoever they listed; likewise shall also the Son of man suffer of them.** *Then the disciples understood that He spoke unto them of John the Baptist* (Matthew 17:11-13).

<u>Jesus Announced the Betrayer</u>. Jesus announced the presence of the betrayer at the last supper when, *He declared,* **The Son of man indeed goes just as it is written of him** (Mark 14:21). It was at the close of the Passover meal, which was evangelized and then superseded and set aside. Much of the doctrine and duty of the Eucharist is illustrated to us by the law of the Passover, for the Old Testament institutions do not bind us. Rather, they instruct us, by the help of a gospel-key to them. *The Son of man goes as it is written* (Mark 14:21).

The Son of man indeed goes, as it is written of him: but woe to that man by whom the Son of man is betrayed! Good were it for that man if He had never been born (Mark 14:21).

<u>Jesus Submitted to Arrest</u>. Later the same evening Jesus submitted to His captors with the words, **The Scriptures must be fulfilled.** He reconciled himself to all the injurious, ignominious treatment by referring himself to the Old Testament prediction of the Messiah. *I am hardly used, but I submit, for the Scriptures must be fulfilled.*

I was daily with you in the temple teaching, and you took me not: but the Scriptures must be fulfilled (Mark 14:49).

<u>Jesus Was Obedient to God, Even Unto Death</u>. We see what a great regard Christ had to the Scriptures. He would bear anything rather than have the least jot or tittle of the word of God fall to the ground. Because He had an eye to them in His sufferings, so He has in His glory, for what is Christ doing in the government of the world, but fulfilling the Scriptures.

<u>Christ is the True Treasure</u>. We must search for Christ, the true treasure hid in the history of the Old Testament. The New Testament expounds the prophecies of the Old Testament, so the

prophecies of the Old Testament illustrate the history of the New Testament.

(3) <u>The Representative Man</u>. "The Son of man" appeared to speak and act in these cases as the representative man. If God had given man dominion over all the work of His hands, then the Son of man in this spiritual Representative sense was in a position to exercise that dominion.

(4) <u>Authority Delegated by God</u>. Jesus used the title "Son of man" to refer to himself as the one who exercised exceptional authority delegated to Him by God. Jesus used the title when he said, ***The Son of man has power (authority) on earth to forgive sins***. Jesus used the example of David to point out how ridiculous the Pharisees' accusations were (1-Samuel 21:1-6).

<u>God Set the Sabbath for Man's Benefit</u>. God derives no benefit from having us to rest on the Sabbath, but we are restored both physically and spiritually when we take time to rest and to focus on God.

Therefore the Son of man is Lord also of the Sabbath. God created the Sabbath for our benefit, not His own (Mark 2:10).

<u>Jesus Used His Authority</u>. Jesus declared His authority. He exercised this authority in a way that made some people criticize Him for acting with the authority of God: "The Son of man is also Lord of the Sabbath." Near the end of His ministry; Jesus spoke of His authority as the Son of man. Jesus declared that men and women ***will see the Son of man coming in the clouds with great power and glory*** (Mark 13:26). He also stated to the high priest and others of the court of Israel, ***You will see the Son of man sitting at the right hand of power, and coming with the clouds of heaven***. He seemed deserted and humiliated as He stood awaiting their verdict. But the tables would be turned when they saw Him vindicated by God as ruler and judge of the world (Mark 14:62).

<u>The Sanhedrin Sought to Keep Their Power and Authority in Israel.</u> The high priest and members of the Sanhedrin should have recognized the Messiah because they studied and knew the

Scriptures thoroughly. Their job was to point people to God, but they were more concerned about preserving their reputation and holding on to their authority. They valued human security more than eternal.

Stephen Saw "The Son of Man." Only once in the Gospels was Jesus referred to as "the Son of man" by someone other than himself. This occurred when Stephen, condemned and sentenced to death by the Jewish Sanhedrin, said he could see "the Son of man standing at the right hand of God." In Stephen's vision, the "Son of man" stood as His heavenly advocate, in fulfillment of Jesus' words: **Whoever confesses Jesus before man, the Son of man also will confess him before the angels of God** (Luke 12:8).

Behold, I see the heavens opened, and the Son of man standing on the right hand of God (Acts 7:56).

Also I say unto you, whosoever shall confess me before man, Him will the Son of man also confess before the angels of God (Luke 12:8).

When Stephen saw the glory of God and Jesus the Messiah standing at God's right hand, his words were similar to Jesus' words spoken before the council.

Jesus said unto him, you have said: nevertheless I say unto you, hereafter shall you see the Son of man sitting on the right hand of power, and coming in the cloud of heaven (Matthew 26:64).

Hereafter shall the Son of man sit on the right hand of the power of God? (Luke 22:69).

Stephen's Vision Supported Jesus' Claim. Stephen's vision supported Jesus' claim and angered the Jewish leaders who had condemned Jesus to death for blasphemy. They would not tolerate Stephen's words, so they dragged Him out and killed him. People may not kill us for witnessing about Christ, but they will let us know they don't want to hear the truth and will often try to silence us.

2. THE SON OF GOD

(1) <u>Jesus Belonged to the Family of David</u>. He was proclaimed as the Messiah from David's line, both before His birth and after His resurrection. Jesus was slow to make messianic claims. The reason for this was that the ideas associated with the messiah in the minds of the Jewish people were quite different from the character and purpose of His ministry. He refused to give them any encouragement. Christ was the Messiah. Jesus was descended from the royal family of David. For centuries the Jewish people had awaited a Messiah who would restore the fortunes of Israel, liberating the nation from foreign oppression and extending His rule over the Gentile nation.

(2) <u>"Son of God at His Baptism</u>." Jesus was Proclaimed the "Son of God" at His baptism. The Spirit descended like a dove on Jesus, and the voice from heaven proclaimed the Father's approval of Jesus as His divine Son.

And there came a voice from heaven, saying, You are my beloved Son, in whom I am well pleased (Mark 1:11).

(3) <u>The Angel Gabriel Named Him "Son of God</u>." He was also given the title by the angel Gabriel at the annunciation: "That Holy one who is to be born will be called the son of God."

And the angel answered and said unto her, the Holy Ghost shall come upon you, and the power of the Highest shall overpower you; therefore also that holy thing which shall be born of you shall be called the Son of God (Luke 1 :35).

(4) <u>Born of the Father</u>. The Gospel of John makes it especially clear that the Father-Son relationship belongs to eternity and that the Son is supremely qualified to reveal the Father because He has His eternal being "<u>in the bosom of the Father</u>." Jesus is God's divine Son in the foundation for all we read about Jesus in the Gospels. We see all three members of the Trinity together: God the Son, and God the Holy Spirit).

"God the One and Only." God communicated through various people in the Old Testament, usually prophets who were told to give specific messages. No one ever saw God. "God the One and only" is a title showing that Jesus is both God and the Father's unique Son. (John 1:18).

Nothing disproves that Jesus is anything other than the Son of the living God.

- In Christ, God revealed His nature and essence in a way that could be seen and touched.

- In Christ, God became a man who lived on earth.

No man has seen God at any time; the only begotten Son, which is in the bosom of the Father, He has declared Him (John 1:18).

3. OUR FATHER

"My Father and Your Father, My God and Your God." Jesus did not link His disciples with Himself in this relationship and speak to them of "our Father" yours and mine. The truth expressed in His words is in John 20:17 which implied throughout Jesus' teachings when He said, *My Father and your Father, my God and your God.*

The Second Coming of Jesus. Mary did not want to lose Jesus. Because she was still struggling with the death of Jesus, she did not yet understood the resurrection. She thought perhaps this was His promised second coming (John 14:3). However, Jesus did not want to be detained at the tomb. If He did not ascend to heaven, the Holy Spirit could not have come. Both Jeus and Mary still had important work to do.

And if I go and prepare a place for you, I will come again and receive you unto myself; that where I am, there you may be also (John 14:3).

Jesus said unto her, Touch me not, for I am not yet ascended to my Father; but go to my brethren, and say unto them, I ascend unto my Father, and your Father, and to my God and your God (John 20:17).

"The Son of Man." As the Son of man in a special sense, Jesus made himself known to the apostle Paul on the Damascus Road. Paul said, *It pleased God to reveal His Son in me.* The proclamation of Jesus as the Son of God was central to Paul's preaching (Acts 9:20; 2-Corinthains 1:19).

According to God's Plan. Because God was guiding His ministry, Paul wasn't doing anything that God hadn't already planned and had given Him power to do. Similarly God guided Jeremiah's life when God called Jeremiah to do a special work (Jeremiah 1:5). God knows you intimately as well, and He chose you to be His even before you were born (Psalm 139). He wants you to draw close to Him and to fulfill the purpose He has for your life.

God Revealed His Son. *But when it pleased God, who separated me from my mother's womb, and called me by His grace, to reveal His Son in me, that I might preach Him among the (Heathen); immediately I conferred not with flesh and blood* (Galatians 1:15-16).

4. MY SON, MY FIRST BORN

"Israel is My Son, My Firstborn." At one level the title Son of God belonged officially to the Messiah, who personified the nation of Israel. *Israel is my Son, my firstborn,* said God to Pharaoh of the prince of the house of David. God declared, *I will make Him my firstborn.* God is sending a message to Pharaoh. The message must be delivered in the name of the great Jehovah: *This said the Lord;* is the first time that God uses this preface which was used frequently afterward by all the prophets. Whether Pharaoh will hear, or whether He will forbear, Moses must tell him, *Thus said the Lord.* Moses must let Pharaoh know Israel's relation to God, and God's concern for Israel.

And this shall you say unto Pharaoh, This said the Lord, Israel is my son, even my firstborn (Exodus 4:22).

It is in the kingdom of the Messiah that this has its full accomplishment, and shall have more and more, when the kingdom of this world shall become the kingdom of the Lord and of His Christ.

And the isles shall wait for His law (Rev. 11:15).

That He should own God as His Father, and God would own Him as His Son, His firstborn (Psalm 89:27).

The Seventh Trumpet of the Revelation. There is no turning back. The coming judgments are no longer partial, but complete in their destruction. God is in control, and He unleashes His full wrath on the evil world that refuses to turn to him. When His wrath begins, there will be no escape. In making note of Revelation we see where the seventh trumpet is sounding the announcing the arrival of the King (Revelation 11:15).

The Seventh Angel of the Revelation. And the rest of the men who were not killed by the plagues repented not of the works of their hands that they should not worship devils, and idols of gold, and silver; and brass, ands tone, and of wood. Neither repented them of their murders, nor of their sorceries, nor of their fornication, nor of their thefts.

And the seventh angel sounded, and there were great voices in heaven, saying, the kingdom of this world is become the kingdoms of our Lord, and of His Christ; and He shall reign forever and ever (Revelation 9:20-21).

5. THE PROMISED MESSIAH

God's Promises Fulfilled in Christ. All of God's promises of what the Messiah would be like are fulfilled in Christ ("I Him it has always been "Yes"). Jesus was completely faithful. He never sinned; he died for us; and now He intercedes for us. Because Jesus Christ was faithful, Paul wanted to be faithful in His ministry.

For the Son of God, Jesus Christ, who was preached among you by us, even by me and Silvanus and Timotheus, was not yea and nay, but in Him was yea. For all the promises of God in Him is yea, and in Him Amen, unto the glory of God by us (2-Corinthians 1:19-20).

God's Promises of What the Messiah Would be Like.

For Christ also has once suffered for sins, the just for the unjust, that He might bring us to God, being put to death in the flesh, but quickened by the Spirit (1-Peter 3:18).

But we see Jesus, who was made a little lower than the angels for the suffering of death, crowned with glory and honor, that He by the grace of God should taste death for every man (Hebrews 2:9).

Who is He that condemned? It is Christ that died, yea rather, that is raised again, who is even at the right hand of God, who also made intercession for us (Romans 8:34).

Seeing then that we have a great high priest that is passed into the heavens, Jesus the Son of God, let us hold fast our profession. For we have not an high priest which cannot be touched with the feeling of our infirmities; but was in all points tempted like as we are, yet without sin (Hebrews 4:14-15).

"The Son of God." When Jesus is present as the Son of God in the New Testament, two aspects of His person are emphasized:

(1) His eternal relation to God as His Father and
(2) His perfect revelation of the Father to the human race.

6. THE WORD OF GOD

The Perfect Relationship Between Jesus and God. The perfect relationship between Jesus and the Father is also expressed when He is described as "the word of God." "The Word" is the self-expression of God; that self-expression has personal status, which exists eternally with God. The word by which God created the world saying, *Let there be light and there was light* (Genesis 1:3). He also spoke through the prophets, "became flesh" in the fullness of time, and lived among the human race as Jesus of Nazareth. What

Jesus taught and what He did are tied inseparably to who He is. John shows Jesus as fully human and fully God.

[1] In the beginning was the Word, and the Word was with God, and the Word was God. [2] The same was in the beginning with God. [3] All things were made by Him and without Him was not anything made that was made. [4] In Him was life, and the life was the light of men, [5] and the light shone in darkness; and the darkness comprehended it not. [6] There was a man sent from God whose name was John. [7] The same came for a witness, to bear witness of the light that all men through Him might believe. [8] He was not that light, but was sent to bear witness of that light (John 1:1-8).

"The Lord of Creation." This is a poetic summary of the first chapter of Genesis. God is not just the coordinator of natural forces He is the Lord of creation, the almighty God. Because He is all-powerful, we should revere Him in all we do.

By the word of the Lord were the heavens made, and all the host of them by the breath of His mouth (Psalm 33:9).

"The One and Only, Who Came From the Father." This means Jesus is God's only and unique Son. The emphasis is on unique. Jesus is one of a kind and enjoys a relationship with God unlike all believers who are called "children" and said to be "born of God."

And the Word was made flesh, and dwelt among us; And we beheld His glory, the glory as of the only begotten of the Father, full of grace and truth (John 1:14).

When Christ was Born, God Became a Man. He was not part man and part God; He was completely human and completely divine according to Colossians 2:9 which says, *For in Him dwell all the fullness of the Godhead bodily.*

Because Christ came, people could know God partially. After Christ came people could know God fully because He became visible and tangible in Christ. Christ is the perfect expression of God in human form. The two most common errors people make about Jesus are to minimize His humanity or to minimize His divinity. Jesus is both God and man.

The Old Testament "Word of God." The Old Testament Word of God is of the wisdom of God. *The Lord by wisdom founded the earth* (Proverbs 3:19).

The Lord by wisdom has founded the earth, by understanding has He established the heavens (Proverbs 3:19).

The New Testament Christ. In the New Testament, Christ is portrayed as

- the personal wisdom of God (Corinthians 1:24-30); and

- the one through whom all things were created (Corinthians 8:6); Colossians 1:16; Hebrews 1:2).

"The Holy One of God." This title was given to Jesus by Peter and also by a demon possessed man.

But He turned, and said unto Peter, Get thee behind me, Satan; You are an offence unto me, for you savor not the things that be of God, but those that be of man (Matthew 16:23).

"The Holy One and the Jesus." In their preaching, the apostles called Jesus "The Holy one and the Jesus."

- This was a name belonging to Him as the Messiah, indicating He was especially set apart for God.

- This title also emphasized His positive goodness and His complete dedication to doing His Father's will.

More "sinlessness," in the sense of the absence of any fault, is a pale quality in comparison to the unsurpassed power for righteousness which filled His life and teaching.

"The Christ, the Son of the Living God." Peter replied on behalf of the rest to the question Christ put to them, as Joshua put Israel to their choice whom they would serve, with design to draw out from them a promise to adhere to him, and it had the like effect. *No, but we will serve the Lord.* Peter was upon all occasions the mouth of the rest, not so much because He had more tongue of His own; and what He said was sometimes approved and sometimes reprimanded. The believing reply which Peter, then Simon Peter answered him, *Lord, to whom shall we go? You have the words of eternal life.*

And we believe and are sure that you are the Christ, the Son of the living God (John 6:69).

7. THE COMMON VIEW OF JESUS

<u>The Disciples Saw Jesus as a Prophet</u>. The disciples answered Jesus' question with the common view that Jesus was one of the great prophets come back to life. This Scripture is a illustration of how some people think and understand the Scriptures. Deuteronomy 18:18, gives the reason the disciples answered Jesus as they did.

According to the word, I will raise them up a prophet from among their brethren, like unto you, and will put my words in His mouth; and He shall speak unto them all that I shall command him (Deuteronomy 18:18).

The disciples didn't understand when God said He would raise up a prophet from among the people. The common profiles they were looking for included John the Baptist, Elijah, and Jeremiah. These were the three prophets they thought Jesus was talking about. After reading the Old Testament, if Jesus were to ask you this same question, how would you answer? Is He your Lord and Messiah?

And Simon Peter answered and said, You are the Christ, the Son of the living God. And Jesus answered and said unto him, Blessed are you, Simon Bajona: for flesh and blood have not revealed it unto you, but my Father which is in heaven (Matthew 16:16-17).

<u>The Spiritual Realm Recognized Jesus as the Messiah</u>. The evil spirit knew at once that Jesus was the Holy one of God. By including this event in Mark's Gospel, He was establishing Jesus' credentials, showing that even the spiritual underworld recognized Jesus as the Messiah.

Saying, Let us alone; what have we to do with you, Jesus of Nazareth? Are you come to destroy us? I know you are the Holy one of God (Mark 1:24).

8. JESUS IS LORD

The most frequent, and most important term in the doctrine of His person, was the Greek word (kurios). It was frequently given to Him as a polite term of address meaning "Sir." Sometimes the title was used of refer to Him in the third person when the disciples and others spoke of Him as "The Lord" or "The Messiah."

Jesus is Lord is the Ultimate Christian Creed. "No one can say Jesus is Lord except by the Holy Spirit." A Christian, therefore, is a person who confesses Jesus as Lord.

Test to Discern False Teachers. Anyone can claim to speak for God. The world is full of false teachers. The Bible gives us a test to help us to discern whether or not a messenger is really from God. The question is: Do they confess Christ as Lord? Don't naively accept the words of all who claim to speak for God. Test their credentials by finding out what they teach about Christ.

Wherefore I give you to understand, that no man speaking by the Spirit of God called Jesus accursed; And that no man can say that Jesus is the Lord, but by the Holy Ghost (1-Corinthians 12:3).

Christ Jesus is the True Messiah and Savior of the World. This proves what you are all bound to believe that Christ Jesus is the true Messiah and Savior of the world. This He closes His sermon with, as the conclusion of the whole matter, the truth to be demonstrated in the book of Acts.

Therefore let all the house of Israel know assuredly that God had made that same Jesus, whom you have crucified, both Lord and Christ (Acts 2:36).

The Title "Lord." The title "Lord" in the Christological sense must have been given to Jesus before the church moved out into the Gentile world. The evidence for this is the invocation "Maranatha" used in the King James Version of the Bible as, "O Lord, come!"

which the apostle Paul, wrote to a Gentile church in the Greek speaking world. The apostle assumed the Gentile world was familiar with the Aramaic. It was an early Christian title for Jesus which was used untranslated. It bears witness to the fact that from the earliest days of the church, the one who had been exalted as Lord was expected to return as Lord.

Looking for that blessed hope and the glorious appearing of the great God and our Savior Jesus Christ (Titus 2:13).

Humble Servant Obedient Even Unto Death. Another key New Testament verse in Philippians shows how Jesus was acknowledged as Lord. In those Philippians verses Paul quoted an early confession of faith. If this is true, he endorsed it and made it his own. This passage tells how Jesus did not regard equality with God as something which He should exploit to His own advantage. Instead He humbled himself and displayed "the form of God" in "the form of a servant." He became "obedient to the point of death, even the death of the cross." God had also highly exalted Him and given Him the *name which is above every name, that at the name of Jesus every knee should bow, and that every tongue should confess that Jesus Christ is Lord* (Philippians 2:5-8; and Philippians 2:9-11).

9. A RELATIONSHIP WITH GOD

We Must Assemble Together. We have significant privileges associated with our new life in Christ:

(1) We have personal access to God through Christ and can draw near to Him without an elaborate system (Hebrews 10:22).
(2) We may grow in faith, overcome doubts and questions, and deepen our relationship with God (Hebrews 10:23).
(3) We may enjoy encouragement from one another (Hebrews 10:24).
(4) We may worship together (Hebrews 10:25).

To neglect Christian gatherings is to give up the encouragement and hope of other Christians. We gather together to share our faith and strengthen one another in the Lord.

Anti-Christian Forces Will Grow in Strength. As we get closer to the "Day" when Christ will return, we *will face many spiritual struggles, and even times of persecution.* Anti-Christian forces will grow in strength. Difficulties should never be excuses for missing Church services. Rather, as difficulties arise we should make an even greater effort to be faithful in attendance to the church.

Keep in mind that every knee shall bow (Isaiah 45:23).

Not forsaking the assembling of ourselves together, as the manner of some is; but exhorting one another and so much the more, as you see the day approaching (Hebrews 10:25).

10. A NAME ABOVE EVERY NAME

Honoring Jesus Glorifies God. In the Old Testament passage of Isaiah 45:23 the God of Israel denies to any other being the right to receive the worship which belongs to Him alone.

I have sworn by myself, the word is gone out of my mouth in righteousness, and shall not return, that unto me every knee shall bow, every tongue shall swear (Isaiah 45:23).

In the passage from Philippians He readily shares that worship with the humiliated and exalted Jesus. More than that, He shares His own name with him. When human beings honor Jesus as Lord, God is glorified. The nations are exhorted to draw near to Jehovah. None beside Him is able to help them; He is the Savior, who can save them without the assistance of any.

If the heart is brought into the obedience of Christ, the knee will cheerfully obey His commands. To Christ men shall come from every nation for blessings. All that hate His cause shall be put to shame, and all believes shall rejoice in Him as their Father and portion. All must come to him. May we now come to Him as the Lord our Righteousness, walking according to His commandments.

<u>"The Word Was God."</u> The Bible presents Christ as altogether God and altogether man. Christ is also the perfect mediator between God and mankind because He partakes fully of the nature of both.

In the beginning was the word and the word was God (Genesis 1:1).

11. MY LORD AND MY GOD

<u>Thomas Called Jesus "My Lord and My God!"</u> This is looking at this in the spiritual sense. If Jesus is called "Lord" in this supreme sense, it is not surprising that He occasionally is called "God" in the New Testament. Thomas was convinced that the risen Christ stood before him. He abandoned his doubts with the confession, *"My Lord and my God!"*

<u>Thomas Doubted but was Still Loyal.</u> It shows that Jesus wasn't hard on Thomas for His doubts. Despite his skepticism Thomas was still loyal to the believers and to Jesus himself. Some people doubt before they believe. If doubt leads to questions, then questions lead to answers, then doubt has done a good work. It is when only doubt becomes stubbornness and stubbornness becomes a lifestyle that doubt harms your faith. When you doubt don't stop there. Let your doubt deepen your faith as you continue to search for the answer.

And Thomas answered and said unto him, My Lord and my God. Jesus said unto him, **Thomas, because you have seen me, You have believed; blessed are you that have not seen, And yet have believed** (John 20:28-29).

<u>The Resurrected Body of Jesus.</u> Jesus' resurrected body was unique. His body was not the same kind of flesh and blood body as Lazarus who was brought back to life. However, Jesus' resurrected body was no longer subject to the same laws of nature as before His death. He could appear in a locked room. He was not a ghost or apparition because He could be touched and could eat. Jesus' resurrection was literal and physical. He was not a disembodied spirit.

12. THE SON OF GOD

<u>Birth of Jesus</u>. In this Gospel, John provides clear evidence that Jesus is the Son of God and that by believing in Him we may Have eternal life. John also provides unique material about Jesus' birth. He did not come into the fullness of his ministry when He was born, but He is eternal.

In the beginning was the Word, and the Word was With God, and the Word was God (John 1:1).

Capernaum became Jesus' home during His ministry in Galilee. Located on a major trade route, it was an important city in the region with a Roman garrison and a customs station.

<u>Importance of the City of Capernaum</u>.

- At Capernaum Matthew was called to be a disciple (Matthew 9:9).

- The city was also the home of several other disciples (Matthew 4:13-19).

- The city was also the home of a high ranking government official (John 4:46).

Although Jesus made this city His base of operations in Galilee, He condemned it for the people's unbelief (Matthew 11:23; Luke 10:15).

He went down to Capernaum, He, and His mother, and His brethren, and His disciples; and they continued there not many days (John 2:12).

CHAPTER 6: WORKSHEET 1
TITLES CONCERNING THE SON OF MAN
(MARK 7; MATTHEW 26; EXODUS 16;
DANIEL 7)

<u>True/False</u>

1. Mark 7 verse _____, *For John the Baptist has come eating no bread and drinking no wine.* T / F

2. Mark Chapter _____ verse34, *Behold, a gluttonous man, and a drunkard, a friend of tax-gatherers and sinners!* T / F

3. Daniel 7:13, *I saw in the might vision, and behold, one like the Son of man came with the clouds of heaven, and came to the ancient of days, and they brought him near before him.* T / F

4. Matthew 26 verse _____, *Jesus said unto him, **you have said: nevertheless I say unto you, hereafter shall you see the Son of man sitting on the right hand of power, and coming in the clouds of heaven**.* T / F

5. In Luke Chapter _____verse 27 it is written, ***And then shall they see the Son of man coming in a cloud with power and great glory.*** T / F

6. In John 1 verse _____, ***Verily, verily, I say unto you, Hereafter you shall see heaven open, and the angels of God ascending and descending upon the Son of man.*** T / F

7. Exodus 16:19, says, *And it came to pass, as Aaron spoke unto the whole congregation of the children of Israel that they looked toward the wilderness, and behold, the glory of the Lord appeared in the cloud* T / F

CHAPTER 6: WORKSHEET 2
TITLES CONCERNING THE SON OF MAN
(MARK 2, 8, 9, 10, 14; ACTS 7:56; EXODUS 19:9)

<u>True/False</u>

1.   Exodus 19:9 W hat did the Lord say unto Moses?

2.   Mark 10:33, *Behold, we go up to Jerusalem.*   T / F

3.   Mark 8:31, *The Son of man must suffer many things.*   T / F

4.   Mark 9:12, *Elias verily came first, and restored all*   T / F
      things.

5.   Mark 9:12, What did Jesus answer and tell them?

      _____

6.   Mark 14:21 says, _____   T / F

      _____

      _____

7.   *I was daily with you in the temple teaching,*   T / F
      and you took me not: but the Scriptures must be
      fulfilled. This is Mark 14:23 or Mark ____: ____

8.   Mark 2:28, *Therefore the Son of man is Lord also*   T / F
      of the Sabbath.

9.   Mark 2:10, *I say unto you, Arise, and take up your*   T / F
         bed, and go your way into your house.

10   Acts 7:56, *And said, behold, I see the heavens*   T / F
         opened, and the Son of man standing on the right
         hand of God.

CHAPTER 7.
THE WORK OF CHIRST

1. THE LORD'S SUPPER

<u>Instructions for Observing the Lord's Supper</u>. We should take the Lord's Supper thoughtfully because we are Proclaiming that Christ died for our sins.

- We should take it worthily with due reverence and respect.

- We should examine ourselves for any unconfessed sin or resentful attitude.

- We are to be properly prepared, based on our belief in and love for Christ.

- We should be considerate of others and wait until everyone is present, and then eating in an orderly and unified manner.

<u>Paul Instructed the Church Members</u>. When Paul said no one should take the Lord's Supper in an unworthy manner, He was speaking to the church members who were rushing into it without thinking of its meaning. Those who did so were *"guilty of sinning against the body and blood of the Lord."* Instead of honoring His sacrifice, they were sharing in the guilt of those who crucified Christ. In reality, no one is worthy to take the Lord's Supper because we all were sinners before being saved by grace.

<u>Preparing Ourselves for Communion</u>. This is why we should prepare ourselves for communion through healthy introspection, repenting and confession of sin, and in resolution of the differences with others. These actions remove the barriers that affect our relationship with God through Christ Jesus as well as with other believers. Having awareness of our sin should not keep us away

from communion but it should drive us to the participation in it by examining ourselves in making ourselves worthy. "*Not recognizing the body of the Lord*" means not understanding what the Lord's Supper means and not distinguishing it from a normal meal. Those who do so condemn themselves.

Wherefore whosoever shall eat this bread, and drink this Cup of the Lord, unworthily, shall be guilty of the body and blood of the Lord (1-Corinthians 11:27).

<u>"Fallen Asleep."</u> Fallen asleep is another way to describe being dead. Some of the people who had died may have had a special supernatural judgment which highlights the seriousness of the communion service. The Lord's Supper is not to be taken lightly. This new covenant cost Jesus His life. It is not a meaningless ritual, but a sacrament given by Christ to help strengthen our faith.

People should come to this meal desiring fellowship with other believers and prepare the Lord's Supper to fellowship, not to fill up on a big dinner. "If anyone is hungry, He should eat at home." This means that they should eat dinner beforehand, so as to come to the fellowship meal in the right frame of mind.

<u>Paul's Instructions for Observing the Lord's Supper</u>. Paul gives specific instructions on how we as Christians should celebrate the Lord's Supper as well as how to observe it.

- We should take the Lord's Supper thoughtfully because we are proclaiming that Christ did for our sins.

- We should take it worthily, with due reverence and respect.

For as often as you eat this bread, and drink this Cup, you do show the Lord's death till He come. Wherefore whosoever shall eat this bread, and drink this cup of the Lord unworthily, shall be guilty of the Body and blood of the lord (1-Corinthians 1:26-27).

Reflect and Examine Your Attitudes.

- We should examine ourselves for any unconfessed sin or resentful attitude toward any one.

- We are to be properly prepared, based on our belief in and love for Christ.

- We should be considerate of others.

- We are to wait until everyone is there and served before eating in an orderly and unified manner.

[28] But let every man examine himself, and so let Him eat that Bread and drink of that cup, [29] For He that eats and drinks unworthily, eat and drink damnation to himself, not discerning the Lord's body; [30]For this cause many are weak and sickly among you, and many sleep; [31] For if we would judge ourselves, we should not be judged. [32] But when we are judged, we are chastened of the Lord, that we should not be condemned with the world. [33] Wherefore, my brethren, when you come together to eat, tarry one for another, [34] And if any man hunger, let Him eat at home; and the rest will set in order when I come (1-Corinthians 11:28-34).

"This is My Body." Christians generally agree that participating in the Lord's Supper is an important element in the Christian faith and that it strengthens us spiritually. There are several different interpretations for what Christ meant when He said, *"This is my body."*

- Some believe that the wine and bread actually become Christ's physical blood and body.

- Others believe the bread and wine remain unchanged, but Christ is spiritually present with the bread and wine.

- Still others believe the bread and wine symbolize Christ's body and blood.

And when He had given thanks He brake it and said, **Take, eat this is my body, which is broken for you. This do in remembrance: of me** (1-Corinthians 11:24).

<u>What is This New Covenant</u>? In the old covenant people could approach God only through the priests and the sacrificial system. Jesus' death on the cross ushered in the New Covenant or agreement between God and man. Now all people can personally approach God and communicate with him.

The people of Israel first entered into this agreement after their Exodus from Egypt (Exodus 24), and it was designed to point to the day when Jesus Christ would come. The new covenant was completed rather than replacing the old covenant, and fulfilling everything the old covenant looked forward to (Jeremiah 31:31-34). Eating the bread and drinking the cup shows that we are remembering Christ's death on our behalf and renewing our commitment to serve him.

After the same manner also He took the cup, when He had supped, saying, ***This cup is the new testament in my blood. This do you, as often as you drink it, in remembrance of me*** (1-Chrinthians 11:25).

<u>The Good News</u>. The Lord's Supper is a visible representation of the Good News of the death of Christ for our sins. He reminds us of Christ's death and the glorious hope of His return.
Our participation in it strengthens our faith through fellowship with Christ and with other believers.

For as often as you eat this bread and drink this cup, you do show the Lord's death till He come (1-Corinthians 11:20).

<u>Paul Condemned Abuse in the Early Church</u>. When the Lord's Supper was celebrated in the early church, it included a feast or fellowship meal followed by the celebration of Communion. In the church in Corinth, the fellowship meal had become a time when some ate and drank excessively while others went hungry. There was little sharing and caring. This certainly did not demonstrate the unity and love that should characterize the church, nor was it a preparation for Communion. Paul condemned these actions and reminded the church of the real purpose of the Lord's Supper.

For in eating every one takes before others his own supper, and one is hungry, and another is drunken (1-Corinthians 11:21).

The Meaning of the Lord's Supper. The early church remembered that Jesus instituted the Lord's Supper on the night of the Passover meal (Luke 22:13-20). Just as the Passover celebrated deliverance from slavery in Egypt, so the Lord's Supper was a celebration of deliverance from sin by Christ's death.

2. THE FIRST WITNESSES

The Work of Christ. The work of Christ has often been stated in relation to His threefold office:

- As prophet of God to the world, He fully revealed God's character and will.

- As priest, Jesus has offered to God by His death a sufficient sacrifice for the sins of the world. On the basis of that sacrifice, He exercises a ministry of intercession on behalf of His people.

- As king, He is "the ruler over the kings of the earth"--the one to whose rule the whole world is subject.

And from Jesus Christ, who is the faithful witness, and the first begotten of the dead, and the prince of the kings of the earth, Unto Him that loved us, and washed us from our sin in His blood (Revelation 1:5).

Only Jesus Rose from the Dead. Others had risen from the dead. During their ministries the prophets, Jesus, and the apostles had brought people back to life but later those people died again in the course of human beings. Jesus was the only one who rose from the dead in an imperishable body, never to die again. He is the firstborn from the dead.

But now is Christ risen from the dead, and become the firstfruits of them that sleep (1-Corinthians 15 :20).

Witnesses to Their Faith. There are many who don't feel the change in their lives has been spectacular enough to witness their faith in Christ. You only qualify as a witness for Jesus because of what

He has done for you, not because of what you have done for him. Christ demonstrated in His death on the cross that he has *freed us from our sin through His blood*, guaranteeing us a place in His kingdom and making us priests to administer God's love to others. The fact that the all-powerful God has offered eternal life to each of us is nothing short of spectacular.

3. THE FINISHED WORK OF CHRIST

<u>The Woman at the Well</u>. Jesus' message was to the woman at the well. She mistakenly believed that if she received the water Jesus offered, she would never have to return to the well each day. It seems that she was just interested in Jesus' message because she thought it could make her life easier. However, if that was always the case, people would accept Christ's message for the wrong reasons. Christ didn't come to take away challenges. Christ came to

- Change us on the inside and

- Empower us to deal with problems from God's perspective.

<u>The Atonement for Man's Sins</u>. The "finished" work of Christ means the work of atonement or redemption for the human race which He completed by His death on the cross. This work is so perfect in itself that it requires neither repetition nor addition. Because of this work He is called "Savior of the World" (John 4:14) and He gives the water so you will never thirst again. He is the "Lamb of God" who takes away the sin of the world.

John saw Jesus coming unto him, and said, behold the Lamb of God, who takes away the sin of the world (John 1:29).

The woman didn't immediately understand what Jesus was talking about. It takes time to accept something that changes the very foundation of your life. Jesus allowed the woman time to ask questions and put the pieces together for herself. Sharing the gospel will not always have immediate results. When you ask people to let Jesus change their lives give them time to weigh the matter.

4. HOW GOD VIEWS SIN

<u>God Views Sin in Several Ways</u>.

- As an offense against God, which requires a pardon;

- As defilement which requires cleansing;

- As slavery which cries out for emancipation;

- As a debt which must be canceled;

- As defeat which must be reversed by victory; and

- As estrangement which must be set right by reconciliation.

<u>Christ Provides the Remedy</u>. It is through the work of Christ that the remedy for sin is provided. Jesus has procured the pardon, the cleansing, the emancipation, the cancellation, the victory, and the reconciliation.

<u>An Altar of Uncut Stone</u>. The Lord specified an altar made of uncut stones (fieldstones) so the people would not begin worshiping the altars as idols. To use a chisel on a stone of the altar would be to profane it. In addition, because the Israelites did not have the capacity to work with iron at that time, using iron tools might mean using the cooperation and expertise of other nations.

Thou shall build the altar of the Lord your God of whole stones, and thou shall offer burnt offerings thereon unto the Lord your God (Deuteronomy 27:6).

Will come unto you, and I will bless thee. And if you will make me an altar of stone, you shall not build it of hewn stone: for if you lift up your tool upon it, you have polluted it. Neither shall you go up by steps unto my altar, that your nakedness be not discovered thereon (Exodus 20:24-26).

<u>A Breach of God's Laws</u>. When sin is viewed as an offense against God, it is also interpreted as a breach of His law. The law of God, like law in general, involves penalties against the lawbreaker. So strict are these penalties that they appear to leave no avenue of escape for the lawbreaker. The apostle Paul argued along these

lines and quoted one uncompromising declaration from the Old Testament: *Cursed is everyone who does not continue in all things which are written in the book of the law, to do them* (Galatians 3:10).

For as many as are of the works of the law are under the curse; for it is written, Cursed is every one that continued not in all things which are written in the book of the law to do them (Galatians 3:10).

<u>The Law Can Only Condemn</u>. Paul's quote of Old Testament Deuteronomy 27:26 proves that, contrary to that which the Judaizers claimed, the law cannot justify and save; it can only condemn. Breaking even one commandment brings a person under condemnation. Because of it everyone that breaks it stands condemned. The law can't do anything to reverse the condemnation.

[20] Therefore by the deeds of the law there shall no flesh be justified in His sight; for by the law is the knowledge of sin. [21] But now the righteousness of God without the law is manifested being witnessed by the law and the prophets; [22] Even the righteousness of God which is by faith of Jesus Christ unto all and upon all them that believe. For there is no difference, [23] for all have sinned, and come short of the glory of God; [24] Being justified freely by His grace through the redemption that is in Christ Jesus (Romans 3:20-24).

<u>Christ Took the Curse of the Law</u>. Christ's death provided a way for all people to come to God. It cleared away the sin that keeps us from having a right relationship with our Creator. This does not mean that everyone has been saved. Instead the way has been cleared for anyone who will trust Christ by faith to be saved. We can have peace with God and be reconciled to Him by accepting Christ who died in our place. Is there is a distance between you and the God who created heaven and earth? If that is true then become reconciled unto him. Come to Him through Christ.

And having made peace through the blood of His cross, by Him to reconcile all things unto himself; by him, I say, whether they are things in earth, or things in heaven (Colossians 1:20).

5. THE COLOSSSIAN HERESY

The heresy was a "mixed bag," containing elements from several different heresies, some of which contradicted each other as shown.

THE COLOSSIAN HERESY:

THE HERESY	REFERENCE IN COLOSSIANS	PAUL'S ANSWER
Spirit is good; Matter is evil	1:15-20	God created heaven and earth for His glory.
One must follow ceremonies, rituals, and restrictions in order to be saved or perfected.	2:11; 16-23 3:11	There were only shadows that ended when Christ came; He is all you need to be saved.
One must deny personal thoughts and desires.	2:20-23	Asceticism is no help in conquering evil thoughts and desires; instead, it leads to pride.
Angels must be worshiped.	2:18	Angels are not to be worshipped. Christ alone is worthy of worship.
Christ could not be both human and divine.	1:15-20 2:2-3	Christ is God in the flesh. He is the eternal one, head of the body, first in everything. Supreme.

THE HERESY	REFERENCE IN COLOSSIANS	PAUL'S ANSWER
One must obtain "secret knowledge" in order to be saved or perfected and this was not available to everyone.	2:2, 18	God's secret is Christ and He has been revealed to all.
One must adhere to human wisdom, tradition and philosophies.	2:4, 8-10 3:15-17	By themselves these can be misleading and shallow because they have human origin. Instead, we should remember what Christ taught and follow His words as our ultimate authority.
It is even better to combine aspects of several religions.	2:10	You have everything when you have Christ. He is sufficient.
There is nothing wrong with immorality.	3:1-11	Get rid of sin and evil because you have been chosen by God to live as a representative of the Lord Jesus Christ.

6. THE DEATH OF CHRIST REDEEMED US

<u>Jesus Offered His Life to God on Behalf of Mankind</u>. In the hour of Jesus Christ's death, He offered His life to God on behalf of mankind. The perfect life which He offered was acceptable to God. The salvation secured through the giving up of that life is God's free gift to mankind in Christ Jesus.

<u>Christ Endured Death</u>. The Bible teaches that Christ, by enduring the form of death on which a divine curse was expressly pronounced in the law, absorbed into himself the curse invoked on the lawbreaker: *Christ has redeemed us from the curse of the law, having become a curse for us for it is written, Cursed is everyone who hangs on a tree.*

<u>Christ Bore Our Sins</u>. This passage is applied to the death of Christ, not only because He bore our sins and was exposed to shame as malefactors who were accursed of God, but because He was taken down from the cursed tree and buried by the particular care of the Jews, with an eye to this law (John 19:31). The guilt being removed, the law was satisfied, as it was when the malefactor had hanged till sun-set; it demanded no more.

<u>Washed and Cleansed</u>. Then He ceased to be a curse, and those that were His. And as the land of Israel was pure and clean when the dead body was buried, so the church is washed and cleansed by the complete satisfaction which thus Christ Jesus made.

- <u>Old Testament</u>: *His body shall not remain all night upon the tree, but you shall in any wise bury Him that day; for He that is hanged is accursed of God; that your land be not defiled, which the Lord your God gave you for an inheritance* (Deuteronomy 21:23).

- <u>New Testament</u>: *The Jews therefore, because it was the preparation, that the bodies should not remain upon the cross on the Sabbath day, for that Sabbath day was an high day, Besought Pilate that their legs might be broken, and that they might be taken away* (John 19:31).

<u>Being Made Sin for Us</u>. Being made sin for us He was made a curse for us; not separated from God but laid for the present under that infamous token of the divine displeasure upon which the law of Moses had put a particular brand (Deuteronomy 21:23). The design of this was that the blessing of Abraham might come on the Gentiles through Jesus Christ that all who believed on Christ, whether it be Jews or Gentiles, would receive that great promise of the Spirit which was peculiarly reserved for the time of the gospel.

<u>Justified In Terms of a Court of Law</u>. In a system of ethics in which acts are morally viewed in terms of a law court, one might speak of the accused party as being "acquitted." The term preferred in the New Testament, especially by the apostle Paul, is the more positive word "justified." Paul goes on to the limit of daring to say that "God justifies the ungodly."

<u>Saved by Our Faith in Jesus</u>. When some people learn that they are saved by God through faith they start to worry whether they have enough faith. They wonder, "Is my faith strong enough to save me?" These people miss the point. It is Jesus Christ who saves us, not our feelings or actions. He is strong enough to save us no matter how weak our faith is.

<u>Salvation Offered as a Gift</u>. Jesus offers us salvation as a gift because He loves us, not because we have earned it through our powerful faith. What, then, is it the role of faith? Faith is believing and turning to Jesus Christ for the forgiveness of our sin, and reaching out to accept His wonderful gift of salvation.

But to Him that work not, but believe on Him that justify the ungodly, His faith is counted for righteousness (Romans 4:5).

<u>Holy Spirit Sent By God</u>. God can be described as Jesus Christ because "Christ died for the ungodly." The Father loved us so much that He sent His Son to bridge the gap between us and God the Father (John 3:16). The Father and the Son sent the Holy Spirit to fill our lives with love and to enable us to live by His power. With all this loving care how can we do less than serve Him completely!

For when we were yet without strength, in due time Christ died for the ungodly (Romans 5:6).

But you shall receive power, after that the Holy Ghost is come upon you: and you shall be witnesses unto me both in Jerusalem, and in all Judaea, and in Samaria, and unto the uttermost part of the earth (Acts 1:8).

7. UNITED BY FAITH

<u>United by Faith and Justified</u>. Those who are united by faith to Him are "justified" in Him. Paul explained that *Christ made Him who knew no sin to be sin for us, that we might become the righteousness of God in him* (2-Corinthians 5:21). When we trust in Christ we make an exchange of our sin for His righteousness. Our sin was poured into Christ at His crucifixion. His righteousness is poured into us at our conversion. This is what Christians mean by Christ's atonement for sin. In the world bartering works only when two people exchange goods of relatively equal value, but God offers to trade His righteousness for our sin--something of immeasurable worth for something completely worthless. How grateful we should be for His kindness to us.

For He has made Him to be sin for us, who knew no sin; that we might be made the righteousness of God in him (2-Corinthians 5:21).

<u>When Sin is Considered Slavery</u>. The work of Christ, seen from this point of view, is to set humanity in a right relationship with God. When sin is considered as slavery from which the slave must be set free, then the death of Christ is spoken of as a ransom or a means of redemption. Jesus himself declared that, **He came to give His life a ransom for many.**

Mark 10:45 reveals not only the motive for Jesus' ministry, but also the basis for our salvation. Paul not only spoke of sin as slavery, he also personified sin as a slave owner who compels his slaves to obey his orders. When they are set free from his control by the death of Christ to enter the service of God, they find His service, by contrast, to be perfect freedom.

For even the Son of man came not to be ministered unto, but to minister, and to give His life a ransom for many (Mark 10:45).

8. THE PENALTY FOR SIN DIED WITH CHRIST ON THE CROSS

The Concept of Sin as Debt. The idea of sin as a debt that must be canceled is based on the teaching of Jesus. In the Parable of the creditor and the two debtors, the creditor forgave them both when they could make no repayment (Luke 7:40-43) even though the debtor owed the larger sum and, therefore, had more cause to love the forgiving creditor. This represented the woman whose *sins were many were forgiven* (Luke 7:47). This is similar to Paul's reference to God as having *canceled the bond which stood against us* with its legal demands.

Blotting out the handwriting of ordinance that was against us, which was contrary to us, and took it out of the way, nailing it to His cross (Colossians 2:14).

Slavery to Sin Died with Christ on the Cross. We can enjoy our new life in Christ because we have joined Him in His death and resurrection. Our evil desires, our bondage to sin, and our love for sin died with him. Joining Him in His Resurrection, we may have unbroken fellowship with God and freedom from sin. Our debt for sin has been paid in full. Our sins are swept away and forgotten by God. We are clean and new. For more study on the difference between our new life in Christ and our old sinful nature, read Ephesians 4:23-24 and Colossians 3:3-15.

Christians Have a New Nature. Before we believed in Christ our nature was evil. We disobeyed, rebelled, and ignored God. Even at our best we didn't love Him with all our heart, soul, and mind. Christians have a new nature. God has crucified the old rebellious nature (Colossians 3:9 and Romans 6:6). The penalty for sin died with Christ on the cross. God has declared us not guilty; we need no longer live under sin's power. Jesus prayed that God would not take us out of the world but to keep us from the evil (John 17:15).

9. HOSTILE FORCES IN THE WORLD

<u>Christ Conquered Death on the Cross</u>. There are hostile forces in this world which have conquered men and women and are holding them as prisoners of war. There was no hope of successful resistance against them until Christ confronted them. It looked as if they had conquered Him too, but on the cross Christ conquered death itself, along with all other hostile forces.

<u>Principalities and Powers</u>. The Bible speaks of the "principalities and powers" as a personification of the hostile forces in the world which have conquered men and women and hold them as prisoners of war. There was no hope of successful resistance against them until Christ confronted them. It looked as if they had conquered Him too, but on the cross He conquered death itself, along with all other hostile forces. In His victory all who believe in Him have a share: *Thanks be to God, who gives us the victory through our Lord Jesus Christ.*

The victory through Jesus Christ, But thanks be to God, which gives us the victory through our Lord Jesus Christ (1-Corinthians 15:57).

Who are these powers and authorities? Several suggestions have been made including

(1) demonic powers,
(2) the gods of the powerful nations,
(3) angels (highly regarded by the heretical teachers), or
(4) the government of Rome.

These powers and authorities were probably not the demonic forces in Colossians 2:10. However, you may now understand why the word probably is being used.

The Bible speaks of the principalities and having spoiled principalities and powers. He made a show of them openly, triumphing over them (Colossians 2:15).

<u>The Worship of Angels</u>. These demonic forces are more likely angels who were mediators of the law (Galatians 3:19). The

Colossian false teachers were encouraging worship of angels. At His death, Christ surpassed the position and authority of any angel. Therefore, rather than fear angels or worship them we are to view them as deposed rulers.

Angels are Not to be Compared to Jesus Christ. While the Bible says the angels are not to be compared to Christ, it isn't saying we should disrespect angels. The Bible says that angels are not to be compared with Jesus Christ (Galatians 3:19).

Power of Rome. Some Bible scholars believe these powers were the powers of Rome. The resurrection of Jesus Christ stripped the power away from a world empire that seemed to temporarily defeat him. This is good for the soul. It is likely the angels were the mediators of the law.

Wherefore then serve the law? It was added because of transgressions, till the seed should come to whom the promise was made; and it was ordained by angels in the hand of a mediator (Galatians 3:19).

10. ALIENATED FROM GOD

The Work of Christ. The present work of Christ begins His exaltation by God, after the completion of His "finished" work in His death and resurrection.

Sin Alienates us from God. Sin is viewed as estrangement or alienation from God. In this case the saving work of Christ includes the reconciliation of sinners to God. The initiative in this reconciling work is taken by God: *God was in Christ reconciling the world to himself.*

To wit, that God was in Christ, reconciling the world unto Himself not imputing their trespasses into them; and has committed unto us the word of reconciliation (2-Corinthians 5:19).

We Have Been Reconciled to God. God brings us back to himself by reconciling us--by blotting out our sins and making us righteous. We are no longer God's enemies or strangers or foreigners to Him when we trust in Christ. Because we have been reconciled to God we have the privilege of encouraging others to do the same and, therefore, we are those who have the "'ministry of reconciliation."

[13] But now in Christ Jesus you who sometimes were far off are made nigh by the blood of Christ; [14] For He is our peace who had made both one, and has broken down the middle wall of partition between us; [15] Having abolished in His flesh the enmity, even the law of commandments contained in ordinances; for to make in himself of twain one new man, so making peace; [16] And that He might reconcile both unto God in one body by the cross, having slain the enmity thereby: [17] And came and preached peace to you which were afar off and to them that were nigh. [18] For through Him we both have access by one Spirit unto the Father. [19] Now therefore you are no more strangers and foreigners, but fellow citizens with the saints, and the household of God (Ephesians 2:13-18).

<u>God Sent Jesus as His Agent</u>. God desires the well being of sinners so He sent Christ as the agent of His reconciling grace to them. Christ's death provided a way for all people to come to God.

And having made peace through the blood of His cross, by Him to reconcile all things unto Himself; by Him, I say, whether they be things in earth, or things in heaven (Colossians 1:20).

<u>Reconciliation Removed Sin</u>. Reconciliation cleared away the sin that keeps us from having a right relationship with God our Creator. This does not mean that everyone has been saved, but that the way has been cleared for anyone who will trust Christ to be saved. We can have peace with God and be reconciled to Him by accepting Christ who died in our place. Is there distance between you and the God of all creation? If so be reconciled to Him today. Come to Him through Christ by asking Him to forgive you. He will do it; He loves you that much.

<u>Estranged from God and from Each Other</u>. Those who are separated from God by sin are also estranged from one another. Accordingly, the work of Christ that reconciles sinners to God also brings them together as human beings. Hostile divisions of humanity have peace with one another through Him. Paul celebrated the way in which the work of Christ overcame the mutual estrangement of Jews and Gentiles: *For He Himself is our*

peace, who has made both one, and has broken down that middle wall of division between us" (Ephesians 2:14).

For He is our peace, who has made both one, and has broken down the middle wall of partition between us (Ephesians 2:14).

<u>Christ Destroyed the Barriers</u>. Some of the many barriers that can divide us from other Christians are age, appearance, intelligence, political persuasion, economic status, race, theological perspective. Christ has destroyed the barriers people build between themselves. Because the walls have been removed, we can have real unity with people who are not like us in Christ Jesus. This is true reconciliation. Because of Christ's death:

- We are all one (Ephesians 2:14);

- Our hostility against each other has been put to death (Ephesians 2:16);

- We can all have access to the Father through the Holy Spirit (Ephesians 2:18);

- We are no longer foreigners or aliens to God (Ephesians 2:19); and

- We are all being built into a holy temple with Christ as our chief cornerstone (Ephesians 2:20-21).

11. THE FIRST WORK OF CHRIST

<u>The Promised Holy Spirit</u>. The first aspect of Christ's present work was to send the Holy Spirit to dwell in His people. *If I do not go away,* He had said to His disciples in the upper room, *the Holy Spirit will not come to you*. Some people take this to mean that Jesus is saying it to us today, it is God who said *I will pour out my Spirit upon the people; but if I depart, I will send Him to you"* (Acts 2:17).

Here Jesus is comforting His disciples because of His imminent departure. *Nevertheless I tell you the truth; it is expedient for you that I go away: for if I go not away, the Comforter will not come unto you; but if I depart, I will send Him unto you* (John 16:7).

The Fulfillment of the Promise at Pentecost. The fulfillment of this promise was announced by Peter on the day of Pentecost: *Therefore being exalted to the right hand of God, and having received it from the Father the promise of the Holy Spirit, He poured out this which you now see and hear* (Acts 2:33).

Therefore being by the right hand of God exalted, and having received of the Father the promise of the Holy Ghost, He had shed forth this, which you now see and hear (Acts 2:33).

John the Baptist Prepared the Way. Although Peter announced the fulfillment of the coming of Christ on the day of Pentecost, John was the first genuine prophet in 400 years. Jesus the Messiah would be infinitely greater than he in his announcement of the coming of Christ. John was pointing out how insignificant he was compared to the one who was coming. John was not worthy of doing the most menial tasks for Him, like tying His sandals. That which John had been, Jesus finished. What John prepared, Jesus fulfilled.

Baptism. John said Jesus would baptize with the Holy Spirit. Sending the Holy Spirit was to live within each believer. John's baptism with water prepared a person to receive Christ's message. This baptism demonstrated repentance, humility, and willingness to turn from sin. This was the beginning of the spiritual process. When Jesus baptizes with the Holy Spirit, the entire person is transformed by the Spirit's power, Jesus offers to us both forgiveness of sin and the power to live for him.

Requests for Spiritual Help are Heard. There are powers and unseen forces of evil in the universe--forces like Satan and the fallen angels. In Christ we are super-conquerors and His love will protect us from any such forces. With Jesus' presence with God we as his representatives receive the assurance that our requests for spiritual help are heard and granted.

<u>It is Impossible to be Separated from Christ</u>. These verses contain one of the most comforting promises in all the Scripture. Christians have always had to face hardships in many forms: persecution, illness, imprisonment, and even death. These could cause them to fear that they have been abandoned by Christ. Paul claims that it is impossible to be separated from Christ. Nothing can stop Christ's constant presence with us. God tells us how great His love is so that we will have the faith that will secure us in Him. If we believe this overwhelming assurance, we will not be afraid.

For I am persuaded, that neither death, nor life, nor angels, nor principalities, nor powers, nor things present, nor things to come (Romans 8:38).

For we wrestle not against flesh and blood, but against principalities, against powers, against the rulers of the darkness of this world, against spiritual wickedness in high places (Ephesians 6:12).

<u>Our Sins are Forgiven</u>. The Book of Hebrews says *that the ever live Jesus Christ is to make intercession* for His people. It describes in detail Jesus' exceptional qualification to be their high priest. No one can add to what Jesus did to save us. Our past, present, and future sins are all forgiven, and Jesus is with the Father as a sign that our sins are forgiven. As a Christian remember that Christ has paid the price for your sins once and for all. That isn't saying you are to go through life sinning just as you please; that won't work because it shows there was no true repentance.

<u>The Enemies of Christ Will be Overthrown</u>. The exaltation of Christ is repeatedly presented in the New Testament as the fulfillment of *the sit at my right hand, till I make your enemies your footstool*. This means that Christ reigns from His present place of exaltation and will do so until His enemies are overthrown. Those enemies belong to the spiritual realm: *the enemy that will be destroyed is death* (1-Corinthians 15:26). With the destruction of death which occurred with the resurrection of Jesus, the present phase of Christ's work gives way to His future work. There are two references concerning this. The first is Psalm 110:1 and the other is 1-Corinthians 15:26).

One of the most-quoted Psalms in the New Testament is Psalm 110 because of its clear references to the Messiah.

A Psalm of David, The Lord said unto my Lord, Sit thou at My right hand, until I make your enemies Your footstool (Psalm 110:1).

The enemy that will be destroyed is death (1-Corinthians 15:26).

Matthew 22:41-45	Jesus recited the works of Psalm 110 and applied them to himself
Psalm 110:1 & 6; Revelation 6-9	Looks forward to Jesus' final and total destruction of the wicked
Psalm 110:2; Revelation 20:1-7	Prophesies the reign of Jesus on Earth
Psalm 110:3-4; Hebrews 5-8	Tell of the priestly work of Jesus for His people
Psalm 110:5-6; Revelation 19:11-21	Look forward to the final battle on earth when Jesus will overcome the forces of evil

<u>Jesus was More than a Teacher</u>. Many people have a belief in God, but refuse to accept Jesus as anything more than a great teacher. But the Bible does not agree. The Old and New Testaments proclaim the deity of the One who came to save and to reign.

- Jesus explained that this psalm spoke of the Messiah as greater than David, Israel's greatest king (Mark 12:35-37)

- Peter used this psalm to show that Jesus, the Messiah, sits at God's right hand and is Lord over all (Acts 2:32-35).

You can't straddle the fence, calling Jesus "Just a good teacher," because the Bible clearly calls Him Lord.

<u>The Future Earthly Work of Christ</u>. During his earthly ministry, Jesus declared that He had even greater works to do in the future. He specified two of these greater works:

(1) Raising of the dead.
(2) Passing of final judgment.

To raise the dead and to judge the world is the prerogative of God who delegated these works to His Son. While the Son would discharge these two functions at the time of the end, they were not unrelated to the events of Jesus' present ministry. Those who were spiritually dead received new life when they responded in faith to the Son of God. In effect, they were passing judgment on themselves as they accepted or rejected the life which He offered.

The last enemy that shall be destroyed is death (1-Corinthians 15:26).

Christ Will Conquer Evil. In this, it is not a chronological sequence of events, and no specific time for these events is given. The Bible points out that the resurrected Christ will conquer all evil, including death (Revelation 20:14).

And death and hell were cast into the lake of fire. This is the second death (Revelation 20:14).

God and Jesus Each Have Work to Do. Although God the Father and God the Son are equal, each has a special work to do and an area of sovereign control (1-Corinthians 15:28). Christ is not inferior to the Father; His work is to defeat all evil. World events may seem out of control and justice may seem scarce but God is in control, allowing evil to remain for a time until He sends Jesus to earth again. Then Christ will present to God a perfect new world.

And when all things shall be subdued unto Him, then shall the Son also himself be subject unto Him that put all things under Him that God may be all in all (l-Corinthians 15:28)

12. THE SECOND COMING OF CHRIST

The raising of the dead and the passing of judgment are associated with the second coming of Christ. The Scripture says that when Paul dealt with this subject, he viewed Christ's appearing in glory as the occasion when His people would share His glory and be displayed to the universe as the sons and daughters of God and heirs of the new order. Jesus also prayed that the ones the Father gave Him would be with Him.

Father, I will that they also, whom you have given me, be with me: where I am; that they may behold my glory, which you have given me: for you love me before the foundation of the world (John 17:24).

Jesus added that all creation looks forward to that time, because then it *will be delivered from the bondage of corruption into the glorious liberty of the children of God* (Romans 8:21).

Because the creature itself also shall be delivered from the bondage of corruption into the glorious liberty the children of God (Romans 8:21).

The Finished Work of Christ. Both the present work of Christ and His future work are dependent on His "finished" work. That "finished" work was the beginning of God's "good work" in His people. This work will not be completed until "the day of Jesus Christ" when the entire universe will be united in Christ.

Being confident of this very thing, that He who has begun a good work in you will perform it until the day of Jesus Christ (Philippians 1:6).

Having made known unto us the mystery of His will according to His good pleasure which He has purposed in himself: That in the dispensation of the fullness of times He might gather together in one all things in Christ, both which are in heaven, and which are on earth; even in Him (Ephesians 1:9-10).

God's Plan is Not a Secret. God was not intentionally keeping His plan a secret (*the mystery of His will*) but His plan for the world could not be fully understood until Christ rose from the dead. His purpose for sending Jesus was to unite Jews and Gentiles in the one body with Christ as the head.

Many People Do Not Understand God's Plan. *When the time is right; when the times will have reached their fulfillment* He will bring us together to be with Him forever. Then everyone will understand on that day. All people will bow to Jesus as Lord, either because they love Him or because they fear His power. This is the concluding work and the ministry of Jesus Christ here on earth.

That at the name of Jesus every knee should bow, of things in heaven; and that every tongue should confess that Jesus Christ is Lord, to the glory of God the Father (Philippians 2:10-11).

13. REMOVING THE CLOUD (John 21-17)

<u>Removing the Cloud of Denial</u>. Jesus led Peter through an experience that would remove the cloud of his denial. Three times Peter had vowed that he would claim or accept Jesus. Three times Jesus asked Peter if he loved Him. When Peter answered "Yes," Jesus told Him to feed His sheep. It is one thing to say you love Jesus but the real test is willingness to serve Him. Peter had repented and Jesus was asking him to commit his life.

Peter's life changed when he finally realized who Jesus was.

- His occupation changed from fisherman to evangelist;

- His identity changed from impetuous to "rock;"

- His relationship to Jesus changed when he was forgiven; and

- He finally understood the significance of Jesus' words about His death and resurrection.

Three times Jesus asked Peter if he loved Him. The first time Jesus said, **Do you truly love me** (Greek agape love; volitional; an act of willingly love; self-sacrificial love). Jesus asked if Peter loved Him more than these? Jesus was seeking something from Peter of greater value.

The second time Jesus focused on Peter alone and still used the word translated into Greek, phileo (signifying affection, or brotherly love) and asked, in effect, "Are you even my friend?" Each time Peter responded with the word translated in Greek as phileo. Jesus doesn't settle for quick, superficial answers. He has a way of getting to the heart of the matter. Peter had to face His true feeling and motives when Jesus confronted him. How would you respond if Jesus asked you, "'Do you truly love me?" Do you really love Jesus? Are you even His friend?

CHAPTER 7: WORKSHEET 1
THE WORK OF CHRIST (PHILIPPIANS 2:10-11; ROMANS 8:21; PSALM 110:1; JOHN 16:9; MARK 1:8

<u>True/False</u>

1. Philippians 2 verse ____. God was not intentionally keeping his plan a secret. T / F

2. Having made known to us the mystery of his will, it wasaccording to his good pleasure. T / F

3. This which he had purposed in himself was a secret. T / F

4. Philippians 2 verse _____*That in the dispensation of the fullness of times he might gather together in one all things in Christ, both which are in heaven, and which are on earth; even in him.* T / F

5. Philippians 2 verse _____ *That at the name of Jesus every knee should bow.* T / F

6. Philippians 2 verse _____ says, *That every tongue should confess that Jesus Christ is lord, to the glory of the Father.* T / F

7. Sin caused all the creation to fall from the perfect state in which God created. T / F

8. Romans 8:21 says, *Because the creature itself also shall be delivered from the bondage of corruption into the glorious liberty of the children of God.* T / F

9.   Psalm 110: 1 says. *The Lord said unto my Lord,*   T / F
      Sit thou at my right hand, until I make your
      enemies your footstool.

10   The first aspect of Jesus' present work to send   T / F
      the Holy Spirit to dwell in H is people.

11.   John 16:9 says, *Nevertheless I tell you the truth,*   T / F
      It is expedient for you that I go away: for if I go not
      away, the Comforter will not come unto you, but if
      I depart, I will send him unto you.

12.   Mark 1:8 says, *I indeed have baptized you with*   T / F
      water: but he shall baptize you with the Holy
      Ghost.

CHAPTER 8.
DAVID, A MAN AFTER GOD'S OWN HEART

1. DAVID, A MAN AFTER GOD'S OWN HEART

Ethical Teachings of Christ. David's moral standards did not reflect the ethical teaching of Christ, even though he wasn't in the world at the time David's time, and yet, he was I God.

In the beginning was the Word, and the Word was with God, and the Word was God (John 1:1).

God Promises to Give us Strength to Meet Challenges. God promises to give us strength to meet challenges, but he doesn't promise to eliminate them. If he gave us no rough roads to walk: and no mountains to climb, and no battles to fight, we would not grow. He does not leave us alone with our challenges; instead he stands beside us, teaches us, and strengthens us to face them.

You have also given me the shield of your salvation: And your right hand has held me up, and your Gentleness has made me great (Psalm 18:35).

David's Glory in Pursuing the War Against the Ammonites (2-Samuel 11:1). We cannot take pleasure in viewing this great action which until we have examined David's achievements, because the beauty of it was stained by sin; otherwise we might not take note of David's wisdom and bravery.

2. SCRIPTURAL REFERENCES TO DAVID

(1) Anointed by Samuel (2-Samuel 5:4-5)
(2) Commits adultery with Bath-Sheba (2-Samuel 11:2-5)

(3) Wickedly causes the death of Uriah (2-Samuel 11:6-25)

(4) Takes Bath-Sheba to be his wife (2-Samuel 11:26-27)

(5) Rebuked by the prophet Nathan (2-Samuel 12:1-6)

(6) David Repents and confesses his guilt (Psalms 4; 6; 32; 38; 51)

(7) Israel chastised with grievous affliction because of David's crime (Psalms 38; 41; 69)

(8) Death of first son born to Bathsheba (2 Samuel 12:15-23; Psalms 27; 66; 122; 144;

(9) Death of David (1-Chronicles 29:26-29)

(10) Charge Delivered to Solomon last words of David (1-Kings 2: 1-11; 1-Chronicles 22:6-19; Chapter 28; Chapter 29)

(11) Sepulcher of age at death (Acts 2:29; 2-Samuel 5:4, Chapt. 5; 1-Chronicles 29:28)

(12) Length of reign, forty 40 years, (1-Kings 2:11; 1-Chronicles 29:27-28)

(13) Wives and Children (2-Samuel 3:23 at Jerusalem; 2-Samuel 5:14-16; 1-Chronicles 3:5-8; 14:4-7)

(14) Descendents (1-Chronicles 3)

(15) Civil and Military Officers (2-Samuel 8:16-18)

(16) Last of his Horses (2-Samuel 23; 1-Chronicles 11; 12:23-40)

(17) David as musician (1-Samuel 16:21-23; 1-Chronicles 15:16; 2-Chronicles 7:5; 2-Chronicles 29:26; Nehemiah 12:36; Amos 6:15.)

(18) Psalms of David, there aren't any reference for this line of David as prophet 1-Samuel 23:2-7; 1-Chronicles 28:19; Matthew 22:41-46; Acts 2:25-28; Acts 4:25.)

(19) Type of Christ (Psalm 2; 16; 69:7-9; Psalms 18:34/43.)

(20) Chronicles written by Samuel, Nathan, and Gad (1-Chronicles 29:29-30)

(21) A prophetic name for Christ, (Jeremiah 30:9; Ezekiel 34:23; 37:24-25.)

3. ANOINTED BY SAMUEL
(1-Samuel 16:13 anointed; 2-Samuel 5:4-5 becomes king).

Then Samuel took the horn of oil, and anointed him in the midst of his brethren, and the Spirit of the Lord came upon David from that day forward. So Samuel rose up, and went to Ramah (1-Samuel 16:13).

[4] David was 30 years old when he began to reign, and he reigned 40 years. [5] In Hebron he reigned over Judah seven years and six months; and in Jerusalem he reigned thirty and three years over all Israel and Judah (2-Samuel 5:4-5).

With the death of Saul came the future to which David had looked since the day of his anointing by Samuel more than 15 years before. The death of Saul and three of his sons left a power vacuum in Judah. David sought the mind of God and was told to go to Hebron where he was formally installed by oil-anointing as king over Judah (2-Samuel 2:1).

And it came to pass after this, that <u>David inquired of the Lord</u>, saying, Shall I go up into any of the cities of Judah? And the Lord said, unto him, Go up. And David said, Where shall I go up? And he [the Lord] said, Unto Hebron (2-Samuel 2:1).
Going to Hebron turned out to be a decisive and important move because it also asserted David's reign as being in rivalry with that of Saul's son, Ishbosheth, who succeeded his father in the North.

<u>Anointed King Over Israel and Judah</u>. David's supporters were convinced that it was time for "the man after God's own heart" to become ruler of the whole nation. After the death of Abner, Saul's commander of Israel's army in the north and Saul's son, Ishbosheth, the way was clear for David to assert his sovereignty over the Northern tribes of Israel as well as over Judah. There was a general recognition in the North that this should be done, so a delegation from all the tribes went to Hebron to encourage David's rule over them.

[1] Then came all the tribes of Israel to David in Hebron, and spoke, saying, Behold, we are your bone and your flesh. [2] Also in time past when Saul was king over us you were he that lead out and brought in Israel; and the Lord said to you, You shall feed my people Israel, and you shall be captain over Israel. [3] So all the elders of Israel came to the king to Hebron; and king David made a league with them in Hebron before the Lord, and they anointed David king over Israel (2-Samuel 5:1-3).

<u>David Oil-Anointed Three Times</u>. Samuel's earlier oil-anointing of David demonstrated God's choice of David. This third

oil-anointing as king over all Israel, like the second oil-anointing as King of Judah, was the people's confirmation of that choice and a public installation.

4. DAVID COMMITS ADULTERY (2 Samuel 11:2-5).

David's Sin with Bathsheba (2-Samuel 11:2). In order to pursue his own sensual pleasures, David left God out of His life and God punished him.

And it came to pass in an evening tide, that David arose from off His bed, and walked upon the roof of the king's house: and from the roof he saw a woman washing herself; and the woman was very beautiful to look upon (2-Samuel 11:2).

Now therefore the sword shall never depart from your house because you have despised me, and have taken the wife of Urish the Hittite to be your wife.

What David said of the mournful report of Saul's death may be applied to the sad story of this chapter in Davis's life--the adultery and murder David was guilty of. "*Tell it not in something amassed, publish it not in the streets of Echelon.* We wish we could draw a veil over it, and that it might never be known nor even be said that David did such things as are here recorded of him.

David Succumbs to Temptation. David's attitude toward Bathsheba should have reflected a godly way of seeing her and not the evil that was done. When you despise the word of God, which is the commandments, it shows that you are being self-centered and not using the ethical teachings of God. One may not fault David for seeking the cooler breezes of the late afternoon, but Bathsheba, knowing the proximity of her courtyard to the palace, probably harbored ulterior designs toward the king. Yet David's submission to her charms is inexcusable, for the deliberate steps he followed to bring her to the palace required more than enough time for him to resist the initial impulsive temptation (2-Samuel 11:2-4).

<u>Identity of Bathsheba</u>. Having discovered that the woman was the daughter of Eliam and the wife of Uriah the Hittite, still David sent for Bathsheba and lay with her. In due time she found that she was pregnant by the king and, undoubtedly in great distress because her adultery would soon become apparent with her husband away in the army, informed him of her condition (2-Samuel 11:4-5)

5. DAVID PLANS MURDER (2 Samuel 11:6-27).

The crisis brought by Bathsheba's pregnancy required some kind of resolution. David sought to legitimize the impending birth by bringing Uriah back from the war siege against the Ammonites so he could visit his wife, Bathsheba. Even though David plied Uriah with wine, Uriah's sense of loyalty to this comrades prevailed over his desire for his wife. Uriah's argument to David was: why should he be allowed the comforts of home and a conjugal visit while his friends in combat were deprived of them? So Uriah refused to visit his wife. Joab was commanding the army at the battle front at the besieged city of Rabbah. David commanded Joab to abandon Uriah to the enemy by an unexpected Israelite withdrawal.

6. DAVID TAKES BATHSHEBA AS A WIFE (2-Samuel 11:26-27).

Bathsheba soon learned of her husband's death, fulfilled the customary time of mourning, then moved into the king's palace in time to bear their son. However, the Lord was displeased and set events in motion that would trouble David until his death.

7. NATHAN THE PROPHET REBUKES DAVID (2-Samuel 12:1-6).

Sometime after the birth of Bathsheba's son, Nathan the prophet told David a story of a rich man who, in spite of having everything, stole a poor neighbor's only female lamb to provide a feast for a guest. David's response was one of rage and he pronounced that the man who would do such a despicable thing ought to die. In addition, David said that the rich man must restore four lambs for the one stolen, because not even the rich man's death could compensate the poor man's loss of property.

It seems easy to see the sins of others without applying the Scriptural standards to ourselves. David called for the full weight of the law to be applied to the person who had done this thing to the poor man because he had no pity.

8. GOD'S PUNISHMENT FOR DAVID AND ISRAEL (2-Samuel 12:7-23).

<u>Nathan's Reply was a Bombshell</u>. Nathan said, *David, You are that man!* Nathan told David that the Lord had given David everything, but David had taken the pet lamb (Uriah's wife) of a poor neighbor. David's punishment would be that he would now suffer the sword as had Uriah and David's wives would be taken from him as Bathsheba had been stolen from Uriah the Hittite. This was fulfilled by David's own son Absalom when he lay with David's concubines (16:11).

<u>Israel Suffers for David's Shame</u>. David's shame would be even greater. While David's shame took place in secret, all these things would happen in the glare of the public eye in broad daylight. Although David could be restored to fellowship with God through genuine and contrite repentance, the impact of his sin remained and would continue to work its sorrow in the nation as well as in the king's life. (Also read Psalms 38; 42; and 69).

<u>Death of Bathsheba's First Son</u> (2-Samuel 15-23). Shortly after Nathan's visit the child became terminally ill. In spite of David's intense fasting and prayer the baby died within a week (2-Samuel 15-23).

<u>Birth of Solomon</u>. The next child born to David and Bathsheba was called Solomon meaning "peace." The Lord through Nathan named him Jedidiah ("loved by the Lord") (2-Samuel 12:24-25).

9. DEATH OF DAVID
(1-Chronicles 29:26-29).

David died very old, very rich and much honored both of God and man. He had been a man of ware from his youth, and as such, had his soul continually in his hand. Yet he was not cut off in the midst of his days but was preserved through all dangers of a military life, lived to a good old age, and died in peace in his bed. These verses bring king Solomon to his throne and king David to his grave.

[26] Thus David the son of Jesse reigned over all Israel. [27] And the time that he reigned over Israel was forty years. . . . [28] And he died in a good old age, full of days, riches, and honor; and Solomon his son reigned in this stead. [29] Now the acts of David the king, first and last, behold, they are written in the book of Samuel the seer, and in the book of Nathan the prophet, and in the book of Gad the seer (1-Chronicles 29:26-29).

He was full of days, riches, and honor. That is, he had enough of this world and of the riches and honor of it but was willing to die and leave it behind. A good man will be full of days, riches, and honor will never be totally satisfied with them because his greatest satisfaction is in God's loving kindness.

But God will redeem my soul from the power of the grave for he shall receive me (Psalm 49:15).

Yea, though I walk through the valley of the shadow of death, I fear no evil, for thou art with me; thy rod and thy staff they comfort me (Psalm 23:4).

This rising generation out of that which went before, and says, "Make room for us." Solomon sat on the throne of the Lord. Not his throne which he prepared in heaven, but the throne of Israel is called the throne of the Lord because not only is he king of all nations, and all kings rule under him, but he was in a peculiar manner king of Israel (1-Samuel 12:12).

10. INSTRUCTIONS TO SOLOMON: LAST WORDS OF DAVID (1-Kings 2:1-11; 1-Chronicles 22 :6-19).

<u>David Counseled Solomon</u>. The first part of David's charge to his son concerned what was of primary importance. David was a realist; he knew he would soon die so he made plans which included counseling his successor. In 1-Kings 2:1-11 Solomon was encouraged to be strong to keep the Word of Lord. He should walk in the ways of the Lord, namely keep His decrees, commands, laws, and requirements because God's blessing depended on His people's obedience to the Law of Moses.

[1] David, that great and good man, is a dying man: The day of David drew nigh that he should die; and he charged Solomon his son, saying, [2] I go the way of all the earth: be strong therefore, and show yourself a man; [3] and keep the charge of the Lord your God, to walk in his ways, to keep his statutes, and his commandments, and his judgments, and his testimonies, as it is written in the law of Moses that you may prosper in all that you do, and whithersoever you turn yourself: [4] That the Lord may continue his word which he spoke concerning me, saying if your children take heed to their way, to walk before me in truth with all their heart and with all their soul, there shall not fail them (said he) a man on the throne of Israel (1-Kings 2:1-4).

<u>No Fear of Death and Dying</u>. The charge and instruction which David gave Solomon when he was dying, he feels himself declining. David is not afraid to hear or speak of dying: *I go the way of all the earth*, (1-Kings 2:2). Death is a but a passage to a better life and world. It is the way of all the earth, of all mankind who dwell on the earth, and are themselves earth, and therefore must return to their earth. Even the sons and heirs of heaven must go the way of all the earth. They must die; but they walk with pleasure in this way, *through the valley of the shadow of death* (Psalm 23:4).

<u>Authority of a Living God</u>. Prophets, and even kings, must go this way to brighter light and honor than prophecy or sovereignty. David is going this way, and therefore gives Solomon directions what to do. David charges Solomon in general, to keep God's

commandments and to make conscience of his duty, (1-Kings 2 :2-4). A good rule to act by the divine will: "Govern yourself by that." David again charges Solomon to keep the charge of the Lord his God. The authority of a dying father is much, but nothing to that of a living God. There are great truths which we are charged with by the Lord our God let us keep them carefully, as those that must give account; and excellent statutes, which we must be ruled by let us also keep them. The written word is our rule. Solomon must himself do as it was written in the Law of Moses. This is a good spirit and reason to act with: *be strong and show yourself as a man*, not only in years but a child as well.

Preparing to Build the Temple. David wanted to build a temple, but God said David was not to build the temple because he was a man of war (1 Chron. 17:4-12). Shedding blood in war was incompatible with building a place of worship. It was left to Solomon, a man of peace to oversee the actual construction. However, David was permitted to prepare plans and materials for the project. The description of these plans are set forth in   1-Chronicles 22:6-19.

Keep the Law of the Lord in Every Way. David also charged Solomon to obey in the matter of the temple and to keep the Law of the Lord in every way. To do so would bring blessing and success. David has also gathered tradesmen skilled in every necessary kind of work. All that was needed was for Solomon to begin the work (1-Chronicles 22:6-19).

David Instructed the Leaders of the Nation. David instructed the leaders of the nation to seek the Lord and also to assist Solomon in every way to build the temple and place within it the holy ark which symbolized the presence of God (1-Chronicles 22:6-19).

11. SEPULCHER OF AGE AT DEATH
(Acts 2:27-30; 2-Samuel 5:4-5; l-Chronicles 29:28)

Peter quoted from Psalm 16:8-11, a psalm written by David. Peter explained that David was not writing about himself, because David died and was buried. Peter tells them in this way:

Men and brethren, let me freely speak unto you of the patriarch David, that he is both dead and buried, and his sepulcher is with us unto this day (Acts 2:29).

Instead, he wrote as a prophet. Peter said, *Therefore being a prophet, and knowing that God had sworn with an oath to him, that of the fruit of his loins, according to the flesh, he would raise up Christ to sit on his throne* (Acts 2:30).

Who spoke of the Messiah who would be resurrected, the audience "decry" to mean the grave. The emphasis here is that Jesus' body was not left to decay but was in fact resurrected and glorified. Peter is says, *Because you will not leave my soul in hell, neither will you suffer you Holy One to see corruption* (Acts 2:27).

[10] So David slept with his fathers, and was buried in the city of David. [11] And the days that David reigned over Israel were forty years: seven years reigned he in Hebron and thirty and three years reigned he in Jerusalem (1-Kings 2:10-11).

[36] For David, after he had served his own generation by the will of God, fell on sleep, and was laid unto his father, and saw corruption [decay of the body]; [37] But he whom God raised again [Jesus], saw no corruption (Acts 13:36-37).

[9] Therefore my heart is glad, and my glory rejoices; my flesh also shall rest in hope. [10] For you will not leave my soul in hell; neither will you suffer your Holy One to see corruption (Psalm 16:9).

1-Chronicles 29:28 again describes David's instructions concerning the temple. Now, with the end of his life imminent, David summoned all the leaders again to encourage them to recognize Solomon's leadership and to follow him in constructing the temple. David concluded his instructions with a charge both to the people and Solomon to keep the divine covenant and to trust God to bring the temple project to a happy fruition.

12. DAVID REIGNS AS KING
(1-Kings 2:11; 1-Chronicles 29:27-28)

David began his reign at age 30, the age at which priests began to serve. After seven and one-half years at Hebron, David decided to relocate the capital. His reason was almost certainly political for he decided on Jerusalem, a city on the border between Judah and the Northern tribes. The distinction between Israel and Judah indicated that 2-Samuel was written after the nation was divided in 931 B.C. into the Northern and Southern Kingdoms (2-Samuel 5:4-5) after the death of Solomon.

And the days that David reigned over Israel were forty years; seven years reigned he in Hebron, and thirty and three years reigned he in Jerusalem (1-Kings 2:11; 1 Chronicles 29:27).

13. DAVID AS MUSICIAN
(1-Samuel 16:21-23; 1-Chronicles 15:16;
2-Chronicles 7:6; 29:26; Nehemiah 12:36;
Amos 6:15.)

<u>Patiently Await God's Instructions</u>. Sometimes our plans even the ones we think God has approved for us we have to be put on hold indefinitely. Like David, we can use this waiting time as well in our life. We can choose to learn and grow in our present circumstance, whatever they may be. Saul's invitation presented an excellent opportunity for young David to gain firsthand information about leading a nation. David went back and forth from Saul.

<u>David Chosen by God</u>. After the seven older sons of Jesse were disqualified one by one by Samuel, David was singled out by the Lord and anointed by Samuel. The anointing, as in the experience of Saul, was accompanied by the coming of the Spirit of God on the boy. As David was invested by the Spirit, that same spirit left Saul. With the departure of the Spirit of God, Saul became tormented by an evil spirit which God permitted to come. In his troubled state Saul could find relief only in music, so he commanded that a musician be found. God arranged that David be the one, so the

shepherd boy was introduced to the palace of the king (1-Samuel Chapter 16:1-14).

[17] And Saul said unto his servants, Provide me now w man that can play well, and bring him to me. [18] Then answered one of the servants, and said, Behold, I have seen a son of Jesse the Bethlehemite, that is cunning in playing, and a mighty valiant man, and a man of war, and prudent in matters, and a comely person, and the Lord is with him. [19] Wherefore Saul sent messengers to Jesse and said, Send me David your son who is with the sheep (1-Samuel 16:17-19).

[21] And David came to Saul, and stood before him; and he loved him greatly. And he became Saul's armor bearer. [22] And Saul sent to Jesse, saying, I pray thee let David stand before me for he has found favor in my sight. [23] And it came to pass when the evil spirit from God was upon Saul that David took a harp and played so Saul was refreshed and was well, and the evil spirit departed from him (1-Samuel 16:21-23).

[13] And the three eldest sons of Jesse went and followed Saul to the battle. . . [15] But David went and returned from Saul to feed his father's sheep at Bethlehem (1-Samuel 17:13, 15).

<u>Musicians Played and Sang when the Temple was Dedicated</u>. When Solomon's Temple was finished, the only object that had not been put in the temple was the ark (2-Chronicles 5:2). Solomon celebrated the transporting of the ark by sacrificing innumerable animals. The priests were joined by Levitical musicians who lifted up their voices and played cymbals, harps, and lyres, (2-Chronicles 7:6; and 29:26) as David had prescribed when he moved the ark to Jerusalem (1-Chronicles 15:15).

And David spoke to the chief of the Levites to appoint their brethren to be the singers with instruments of music, psalteries and harps and cymbals, sounding, by lifting up the voice with joy (1-Chronicles 15:16).

14. PSALMS OF DAVID

There aren't any references for this line of David as prophet (1-Samuel 23:2-7; 1-Chronicles 28:19; Matthew 22:41-46; Acts 2:25-28; Acts 4:25.)

David Sought the Lord's Guidance. David sought the Lord's guidance before he took action. He listened to God's directions and then proceeded accordingly. Rather than trying to find God's will after the fact or having to ask God to undo the results of a hasty decision, we should take time to discern God's will beforehand. His Word and the leading of his Spirit in our hearts, as well as through circumstances.

[2] Therefore <u>David inquired of the Lord</u>, saying, Shall I go and smite these Philistines? And The Lord said to David, Go and smite the Philistines, and save Keilah. . . . [5] So David and his men went to Keilah, and fought with the Philistines, and brought away their cattle, and smote them [the cattle] with a great slaughter. So David saved the inhabitants of Keilah (1-Samuel 23:2-7).

And it came to pass after this, that <u>David inquired of the Lord</u>, saying, Shall I go to any of the cities of Judah? And the Lord said, to him, Go. And David said, Where shall I go? And he [the Lord} said, To Hebron (2-Samuel 2:1).

All this, said David, <u>the Lord made me understand in writing by his hand upon me</u>, even all the works of this pattern (1-Chronicles 28:19).

*[41] While the Pharisees were gathered together, Jesus asked them, [42] Saying, **What think you of Christ: Whose son is He?** They said unto Him, The Son of David. [43] He said to them, **How then does David in spirit call him Lord, saying, [44] The Lord said to my Lord, Sit on my right hand, until I make your enemies your footstool?** [45] If David then call him Lord, how is he his son? [46] And no man was able to answer him a word, neither does any man from that day forth ask him any more questions* (Matthew 22:41-46).

[25] For David spoke concerning him, I foresaw the Lord always before my face, for he is on my right hand, that I should not be moved. [26] Therefore did my heart rejoice, and my tongue was glad; moreover also my flesh will rest in hope [27] because you will not leave my soul in hell, neither will you suffer your Holy One to see corruption [decay of the body]. [28] You have made known to me the ways of life. You shall make me full of joy with your countenance (Acts 2:25-28).

Who by the mouth of your servant David has said, Why did the heathen rage and the people imagine vain things? (Acts 4:25).

15. TYPE OF CHRIST
(Psalm 69:7-9; Psalm 18:34)

[7] Because for your sake I have born reproach; shame has covered my face. [8] I am become a stranger to my brethren, and an alien to my mother's children (Psalm 69:7-9).

[34] He teaches my hands to war so that a bow of steel is broken by my arms. [35] You have also given me the shield of your salvation: And your right hand has held me up, and your Gentleness has made me great (Psalm 18:34-35).

Jeremiah's Reference to King David means the Messiah. Like Isaiah, Jeremiah associated events of the near future and those of the distant future. Reading these prophecies is like looking at several mountain peaks in a range. From a distance they look as though they are next to each other, when actual fact they are miles apart. Jeremiah presents near and distant events as if they will happen soon. He sees the exile, but he sees also the future day when Christ will reign forever. The reference to David is not as King David, but to his descendant, the Messiah.

But they shall serve the Lord their God, and David their king, whom I will raise up unto them (Jeremiah 30:9)

And hath raised up an horn of salvation for us in the house of his servant David (Luke 1:69).

The Perfect Shepherd. In contrast to the present evil shepherd leaders of God's people, God will send a perfect shepherd, the Messiah ("my servant David") who will take care of every need his people have and set up a kingdom of perfect peace and justice. "Peace" means more than the absence of conflict. It is contentment, fulfillment, and security. (Psalm 23; Jeremiah 23:5-6; John 10:11; Hebrews 13:20-21; Revelation 21).

The Lord is my shepherd; I shall not want (Psalm 23).

[5] Behold, the days come, said the Lord, that I will raise unto David a righteous Branch, and a King shall reign and prosper, and shall execute judgment and justice in the earth. [6] In his days Judah shall be saved, and Israel shall dwell safely; and this is his name whereby he shall be called, THE LORD OUR RIGHTEOUSNESS (Jeremiah 23:5-6).

Jesus said, **I am the good shepherd; the good shepherd gives his life for the sheep** (John 10:11).

[20] Now the <u>God of peace</u> *that brought again from the dead our Lord Jesus, that great shepherd of the sheep through the blood of the everlasting covenant, [21] Make you perfect in every good work to do his will, working in you that which is well pleasing in his sight, through Jesus Christ to whom be glory for ever and ever* (Hebrews 13:20-21).

<u>David was Good King</u>. David was a good king, but the Messiah would be the perfect king.

And I will set up one shepherd over them, and he shall feed them, even my servant David; he shall feed them, and he shall be their shepherd (Ezekiel 34:23).

And David my servant shall be king over them; and they all shall have one shepherd. They shall also walk in my judgments and observe my statutes (Ezekiel 37:24).

These shall make war with the Lamb and the Lamb shall overcome them, for he is Lord of Lords, and King of Kings. And they that are with him are called the chosen and the faithful (Revelation 17:14).

CHAPTER 8: WORKSHEET 1
DAVID, A MAN AFTER GOD'S OWN HEART

ANOINTED BY SAMUEL (1-Samuel 16:13; 2-Samuel 5:4-5

1.   1-Samuel 16:13. *Then*

_____ *took the horn*
of _____ *and anointed him in the midst of*
this brethren, and the _____
of the Lord came upon David from that day
forward.

2.   2-Samuel 5:4. David was 30_____ or
40_____ years old when began to
reign.

3.   2-Samuel 5:5. David reigned in
_____ over Judah 7-1/2
years.

4.   2-Samuel 5:5. David reigned in
_____ 33 years over all
Israel and Judah.

5.   Samuel's oil-anointing of the boy David   T / F
demonstrated God's choice of David.

6.   The other oil-anointings as King of Judah   T / F
and later of Israel and Judah were the
people's confirmation of that choice and a
public installation.

DAVID COMMITS ADULTERY (2-Samuel 11:2-5)

7.   2-Samuel 11:verse ____ states that David
committed adultery with Bathsheba.

8. 2-Samuel 11:verse _____ says that Bathsheba sent word to David that she was with child.

DAVID COMMITS MURDER (2-Samuel 11:6-27)

9. 2-Samuel 11:9. Uriah went down to his house to eat, drink, and lie with his wife.   T / F

10. 2-Samuel 11:15. David wrote a letter to the army commander to send Uriah to the battle front so that he could improve his fighting skills.   T / F

11. 2-Samuel 11: verse_____. *And when the wife of Uriah heard that her husband was dead, she _____ for her husband.*

12. 2-Samuel 11: verse_____. When the mourning was past, David took Bathsheba to his house; she became his _____, and bore him a _____.

13. 2-Samuel 11:27. God was pleased with the way David worked things out.

CHAPTER 8: WORKSHEET 2
NATHAN THE PROPHET REBUKES DAVID
(2-Samuel 12:1-20)

1.   2-Samuel 12:1. God sent Nathan the prophet to   T / F
     confront David.

2.   2-Samuel 12: 2-3. There were two men in one   T / F
     city. The rich man had many flocks and herds.
     The poor man had one ewe lamb that was
     loved and treated like one of his children.

3.   2-Samuel 12:verse _____. The rich man   T / F
     took the poor man's <u>lamb / goat</u> and had it
     prepared as a meal to feed a traveler in the
     rich man's house.

4.   2-Samuel 12:verse_____. Upon hearing   T / F
     the story, David's anger was greatly kindled
     against <u>the rich man / Nathan</u>.

5.   2-Samuel 12:verse _____. <u>David / Nathan</u>
     judged that not only should the rich man die
     for the crime but also restore the lamb <u>three-
     fold / four-fold</u> because he had no pity.

6.   2-Samuel 12:7. *And Nathan said to David, You*   T / F
     are the man.

7.   2-Samuel 12:7-8. Nathan listed the ways God   T / F
     had blessed and protected David.

8.   2-Samuel 12:10. *Now therefore the <u>sword / staff</u>*
     shall never depart from your house because you have
     despised me, and have taken the <u>wife / daughter</u> of
     Uriah to be your <u>wife / concubine</u>.

9.   2-Samuel 12:15. One of the punishments for   T / F
     David's evil was the death of the babe born to
     Bathsheba.

DEATH OF KING DAVID (1-Chronicles 29:26-29)

10   1-Chronicles 29:26. David the son of _____
     reigned over all _____.

11. When David died he was full of days, riches, and _____.

12. David's son _____ reigned after David.

13. The acts of David the king are written in the book of _____ the seer, and in the book of Nathan the _____ and in the book of Gad the seer.

14. The time that David reigned over Israel was <u>40 / 50</u> years.

CHAPTER 8: WORKSHEET 3
TYPE OF CHRIST

1. Jeremiah 30:verse 2 _____ or 9____. *But they shall serve the Lord their God, and David their king, whom I will raise up unto them.*

2. Luke 1:69 says, *And hath raised up an horn of salvation for us in the house of his servant David.*   T / F

3. Psalm 23; Jeremiah 23:5-6; John 10:11; Hebrews 13:20-21; Revelation 21
    In contrast to the present evil shepherd leaders of God's people, God will send a perfect shepherd, the _____ ("my servant David") who will take care of every need his people have and set up a _____ of perfect peace and justice.

4. Psalm 23; Jeremiah 23:5-6; John 10:11; Hebrews 13:20-21; Revelation 21   T / F
    "Peace means more than the absence of conflict. It is contentment, _____ and security.

5. Ezekiel 34:23 says, *And I will set up one shepherd over them, and he shall feed them, even my servant David; he shall feed them, and he shall be their shepherd.*   T / F

6. Ezekiel 34:23. The Messiah was often called David because he was David's descendant.   T / F

7. Ezekiel 34:23. David was a good king, but the Messiah would be the perfect king.   T / F

8.   Ezekiel 37:24 says, And David my servant shall be king over them; and they all shall have one shepherd. They shall also walk in my _____ and observe my _____.

9.   Revelation 17:14 says, These shall make war with the Lamb and the Lamb shall overcome them, for he is Lord of Lords, and King of Kings. And they that are with him are called the _____ and the _____.

CHAPTER 8: WORKSHEET 4
PETER AND DAVID
2-Samuel 11:15-23; John 21:15-17

1. Jesus led Peter through an experience that would remove the cloud of his denial. There was a difference between the wrong David did and what Peter did; one sin was greater than the other. T / F

2. The first time Jesus asked Peter did he love him, Jesus called him by name T / F

3. What name did Jesus use in calling Peter? T / F

4. Jesus ask Peter did he love him more than these? T / F

5. John 21: verse _____ Jesus said, *Peter say yea, Lord, you know that I love you* T / F

6. What did Jesus ask Peter to do?
John 21: verse_____ T / F

7. Jesus used a name the second time he asked Peter if he loved him. T / F

8. Again Peter said, *Yea Lord you know I do.* T / F

9. John 20:6. Jesus asked Peter to feed his lambs. T / F

10 The third time Jesus asked Peter did he love him, Peter got angry with Jesus because he asked the same question. T / F

11. Peter knew that Jesus knew everything and all things that could have made him angry T / F

12. Peter knew that Jesus knew him is what made him grieved because Jesus ask the third time. T / F

13. *Lord, you know all things; you know that I love you, then Jesus said unto him, feed my sheep.* This is John 21:17 T / F

CHAPTER 8: WORKSHEET 5
PETER AND DAVID
2-Samuel 11:15-23; John 21:15-17

1.	We have to do or go according to our feelings concerning what Jesus expects of us?	T / F
2.	We do things from a spiritual point of view by faith and what we believe	T / F
3.	How would you respond if Jesus asked you, "Do you truly love him? Are you even his friend?	T / F
4.	We all know there is no big or littler sin	T / F
5.	David's sin was greater than Peter's sin?	T / F
6.	That which David had done was despised the commandments of God.	T / F
7.	Peter rejected the commandments of God.	T / F
8.	Davis rejected the commandments of God.	T / F
9.	One commandment David broke was should not murder.	T / F
10	One commandment David broke was it you committing adultery.	T / F
11.	In the Scripture will find the ten commandments is it the Old Testament.	T / F
12.	Deuteronomy 10:4 ____ or 10:1-11____. the law which was to keep the children free from sin according to the first law.	T / F
13.	When God gave Israel the law in writing, as a standing pledge of his favor	T / F
14.	Deuteronomy 10: 1,2. Although the tablets that were first written were broken, because Israel had broken the commandments, God wrote another table of commandments.	T / F
15.	Peter's sin greater than David's sin	T / F
16.	John 21:15 Jesus asked Simon, son of Jonas, if he loved him more than these.	T / F

17.   John 21:17. Peter became grieved because   T / F
Jesus said to him the third time, Do you love
me? This was a sin.

18.   Adultery is a greater sin than Peter being   T / F
grieved because of being asked three times
did he love Jesus.

CHAPTER 8: WORKSHEET 6
PETER AND DAVID (2-Samuel 11:15-23; John 21:15-17)

1. When does being grieved become sin--Before you act or after you have made an act?   T / F

2. You shall not murder is one of the Ten Commandments.   T / F

3. You shall not commit adultery is one of the Ten Commandments.   T / F

4. Neither shall you bear false witness against your neighbor is one of the Ten Commandments.   T / F

5. 2-Samual 12: verse _____ The Lord struck the child of David which he had by Bath-Sheba in adultery. The child very sick true   T / F

6. 2-Samuel 12: verse _____. David not eat at all and lay all night upon the earth   T / F

7. 2-Samuel 12: verse _____. Servants talked to David in a way of trying to comfort him concerning the death of his child   T / F

8. David ate with the elders.   T / F

9. 2-Samuel 12:15-23. These verses relate the death of David' s first son born from Bath-Sheba   T / F

10. When David was anointed as a boy, he received the _____ of God.1-Samuel 16:verse _____.

11. With the departure of the Spirit of God, Saul became tormented by an evil spirit.

12. In his troubled state Saul could find relief only in _____.

13. 1-Samuel 16:19. Saul sent for Jesse's son, _____.

14. 1-Samuel 16:23. And it came to pass when the evil spirit from God was upon Saul that David took a _____ and played so Saul was refreshed and well.

15. David returned from Saul to feed his father's sheep at _____.1-Samuel 17: verse _____

16. 2-Chronicles 5:2. When Solomon's temple was finished, the _____ of the Covenant still had to be place in the temple.

17. 2-Chronicles 7:6. And the priests waited on their offices: the Levites also with instruments of _____ of the Lord, which David the king had made to 18. praise the Lord.

CHAPTER 8: WORKSHEET 1
ADAM AND EVE (GENESIS 2)

1. Genesis 2:5 says, The Lord God had not caused it to rain upon the earth.   T / F

2. The Lord God said there was not a man to till the ground. Book_____ Chapter _____ Verse_____   T / F

3. The Lord God formed man out of the dust of the ground. Book_____ Chapter _____ Verse_____   T / F

4. Book_____ Chapter _____ Verse 7 says man became a living soul.   T / F

5. Genesis 2:9 says, every tree pleasant to the sight, and good for food.   T / F

6. In the midst of the garden was the tree of life and the tree of knowledge of good and evil.   T / F

7. Book_____ Chapter _____ Verse_____, *The Lord God commanded the man, saying, of every tree of the garden you may freely.*   T / F

8. Genesis 2: Verse_____. *And the Lord God said, it is not good that the man should be alone.*   T / F

9. Genesis 2:18 says the Lord said he would make man a helper for him   T / F

10. Genesis 2:20. Adam didn't want to give names to any of the creations of the Lord God   T / F

11. Genesis 2:20. Because there wasn't a helper for Adam gave him reason to not name the cattle, fowl of the air, and to every beast of the field, Adam was angry because of that.   T / F

21. God forms and equips men and women for various tasks, but all these tasks lead to the same goal which is to honoring God. Man gives life to woman, woman gives life to the world.   T / F

13.   Each role carries exclusive privileges; there   T / F
         is no room for thinking that one sex is more
         superior to the other.

14.   Genesis 2:21. God caused a deep sleep to fall   T / F
         upon Adam because Adam was tired from
         working with the creation of God.

15.   Genesis 2: verse ____. The rib, which the Lord   T / F
         God had taken from man, and made he a
         woman, and brought her unto the man.

CHAPTER 8: WORKSHEET 2
ADAM AND EVE (GENESIS 2 and 3)

1. Genesis 2: verse _____. Adam say this is now bone of my bone, and flesh of my flesh   T / F

2. Genesis 3:5. God says that in the day Adam eat thereof his eyes shall be opened.   T / F

3. Genesis 3: 4_____ or 6_____. The woman saw that the tree was good for food, and that it was pleasant to the eyes.   T / F

4. God gave marriage as a gift to Adam and Eve.   T / F

5. There are three basic aspects: [l] the man must leave his parents.   T / F

6. [2] In a public act, promises himself to his wife.   T / F

7. The man and woman are joined together by taking responsibility for each other's welfare and by loving the mate above all others.   T / F

8. The two become one flesh in the intimacy and commitment of sexual union that is reserved for marriage.   T / F

9. Strong marriage include all three of these aspect.   T / F

10. Genesis 3:7. the eyes of them both were opened, and they knew that they were naked; and they sewed fig leaves together, and made themselves aprons.   T / F

11. Genesis 3:9. The Lord God didn't called out unto Adam and ask, 'What are you doing?'   T / F

12. Genesis 3: verse 5_____, 10_____ or 13_____. The serpent beguiled me.   T / F

13. Genesis 3: verse_____. God cursed the serpent,   T / F

14. Genesis 3:15. God said he would put enmity between your seed and her seed). Who was he talking to?_____   T / F

15. Genesis 3: verse_____. God said it shall bruise your head, and you shall bruise his heel.   T / F

CHAPTER 8: WORKSHEET 3
ADAM AND EVE (GENESIS 2 and 3)

1. Adam and Eve's disobedience and fall from God's gracious presence affected all creation. T / F

2. Years ago people thought nothing of polluting streams with chemical wastes and garbage. T / F

3. Now we know that just two or three parts per million of certain chemicals can damage human health. T / F

4. Genesis 3:17. God said unto Adam, because you have listened to the voice of your wife, and have eaten of the tree, of which I commanded you saying 'You shall not _____ _____,' cursed is the _____for your sake; in _____shall you _____ all the days of your _____. T / F

5. Genesis 3:19. In the sweat of your _____ shall you _____ until you return unto the_____; for out of it was you _____;. for you are _____ unto _____ shall he return to_____. T / F

6. What did God make for Adam and Eve? T / F

7. Out of what did God make coats for Adam? T / F

8. Genesis 3:22. Because man has become as one of _____ God said now, lest he put forth his hands and _____ and _____. T / F

9. Genesis 4:1. Adam knew his wife Eve, and she conceived, and bare Cain and said, I have gotten son from the Lord. The context of this verse refers to the "knowledge" of sexual relationship. T / F

10   Is this child the image of his father
_____ or is he the image of God_____.
Book_____ Chapter _____
Verse_____

11.   The tree of knowledge in verses 1,17, and   T / F
25. Then replace of a son by "knowing" the
murder, which is denied in verse 9 by, "I
know not."

12.   Genesis 3:24 God drove out the man from
the garden and placed _____
turning _____

13.   Genesis 3:24 For what reason   T / F

CHAPTER 8: WORKSHEET 4
ADAM AND EVE (GENESIS 2, 3, 4)

1. Genesis 3:24. This is showing that Adam and Eve broke their relationship with God. T / F

2. They became convinced their way was better than God's. T / F

3. They became self-conscious and hid. T / F

4. They tried to excuse and defend themselves. T / F

5. To build a relationship with God we must reverse those steps. T / F

6. We must drop our excuses and self-defenses. T / F

7. We must stop trying to hide from God. T / F

8. We must become convinced that God's way is better than our way. T / F

9. No longer was everything provided for Adam and Eve as it was in the Garden of Even, where their daily tasks were refreshing and delightful after the fall. T / F

10 Cain became a farmer, while Abel was a shepherd T / F

11. In part of the Middle East to day, these ancient occupations are still practiced much as they were in Cain and Abel's time it seems like. T / F

12. Genesis 4:2. And she again bared his brother Abel. And Abel was a keeper of sheep, but Cain was a tiller of the ground. T / F

13. THE HAND OF A MEDIATOR: Galatians 3:19 Wherefore then serve the law? It was added because of transgressions, till the seed should come to whom the promise was made; and it was ordained by angels in the hand of a mediator. Are we to serve the law. T / F

14. We are to serve the law of God and live by faith T / F

    We please God by serving him by the law. T / F

We are to serve him by faith   T / F

Adam served God by faith during the creation   T / F
after God put Adam. to sleep and taken a rib
from him to make the woman
Book_____ Chapter _____
Verse_____

Adam had children after God put him out of   T / F
the Garden of Eden

God sent Adam forth because he wouldn't put   T / F
forth his hand and take the tree of life and eat
and life for ever

CHAPTER 8: WORKSHEET 5
ADAM AND EVE (GENESIS 2, 3, 4)
REVELATION 22:2; Ezekiel 47:12

1.	In the midst of the street of it, and on either side Of the river, was there the tree of life, which Bare twelve manners of fruits, and yielded her Every month: and the leaves of the tree were for The healing of the nations,	T / F
2.	This tree of life is like the other trees in the Garden of Eden	T / F
3.	And out of the ground made the Lord God to grow every tree that is pleasant to the sight, and good for food	T / F
4.	Genesis 2:9. The tree of life also in the: midst of the garden, and the tree of knowledge of good and evil	T / F
5.	After Adam and Eve sinned, they were forbidden to eat from the tree of life because they could not have eternal life as long as they were under sin's control	T / F
6.	After Adam was forbidden he disobeyed God and sinned, when he put forth his hand, and took also the tree of life. Book_____ Chapter ____ Verse___	T / F
7.	Because of the forgiveness of sin through the blood of Jesus Christ, there will be no evil or sin in this city John is talking about	T / F
8.	We will able to eat freely from the tree of life	T / F
9.	When sin's control over us is destroyed and our eternity with God is secure.	T / F
10	Why would the nations need to be healed if all evil is gone?	T / F

11.   John is quoting something from Ezekiel that   T / F
        you might like to read, where water flowing
        from the temple produces trees with healing
        leaves.

12.   John is quoting something from Ezekiel that   T / F
        you might like to read, where water flowing
        from the temple produces trees with healing
        leaves.
        Book_____   Chapter   _____
        Verse____

13.   Ezekiel 47:12. And by the river upon the   T / F
        bank thereof, on this side and on that side,
        shall grow all trees for meat, whose leaf
        shall not fade, neither shall the fruit thereof
        be consumed: it shall bring forth new fruit
        according to his month, because their waters
        they issued out of the sanctuary: and the fruit
        thereof shall be for meat, and the leaf thereof
        for medicine.

CHAPTER 8: WORKSHEET 6
ADAM AND EVE (GENESIS 2, 3, 4)
REVELATION 22:2; Ezekiel 47:12

1. What was the tree of knowledge called?   T / F

2. What was good and evil called in the Garden   T / F
    of Eden?

3. The name of the tree of the knowledge of   T / F
    good and evil, implies that evil has already
    occurred.

4. If not in the garden, then could it have been   T / F
    during the time of Satan's fall.

5. Were the tree of life and the tree of the   T / F
    knowledge of good and evil real? There are
    two views are often expressed:
    (1) The tree was real, but symbolic. Eternal
    life with God was pictured as eating from the
    tree of life.

6. (2) The tree was real, possessing special   T / F
    properties which is owned by God meaning
    God is ownership of that which is spiritual

7. By eating the fruit from the tree of life, Adam   T / F
    and Eve could have had eternal life, enjoying
    a permanent relationship as God's children,
    which could not happen

8. (3) In either case, Adam and Eve's sin separated   T / F
    them from the tree of life and kept them from
    obtaining eternal life.

9. The tree of life again appears in a description   T / F
    in Revelation 22:2 where people enjoyed
    eternal life with God.

10 Genesis 3:9. God called out unto Adam. asking   T / F
    'Where are you?'

11. Adam said he hid himself because he didn't   T / F
    want to see God

12. Adam said he heard God's voice in the garden,   T / F
    and he was afraid, because he was naked; and
    he hid himself

13. Genesis 3:12-13. God said unto the woman,   T / F
    what is this that you have done? And the
    woman said the _____beguiled
    me, and I did _____. The woman said
    unto _____ we may eat of the
    fruit of the _____of the garden.

14. Genesis 3:2. The serpent a creature made by   T / F
    God but used by Satan.

CHAPTER 8: WORKSHEET 7
ADAM AND EVE (GENESIS 2, 3, 4)
REVELATION 22:2; Ezekiel 47:12

The question was asked if the serpent was a creature made by God bus used by Satan. Satan still uses people to obstruct God's work. They may not be conscious of this but their hatred of truth, this is the way some are. Their lies and murderous intentions indicated how much control the devil had over them. They were his tools. They spoke the very same language of lies.

You are of your father the devil, and the lust of your father you will do. He was a murderer from the beginning, and abode not in the truth, because there is no truth in him. When he speaks a lie, he speaks of his own: for he is a Liar, and the father of it (John 8:44).

And Cain talked with Abel his brother: and it came to Pass, when they were in the field, that Cain rose up Against Abel his brother and slew him. He was of his father the devil (Genesis 4:8.)

Wherefore, as by one man sin entered into the world, and death by sin; and so death passed upon all men, for that all have sinned (Romans 5:12.).

Not as Cain, who was of that wicked one, and slew his brother. Wherefore slew he him? Because his own works were evil, and his brother's righteous (1-John 3: 12.)

Genesis 3: 15. *Wherein God said he would put enmity between thee and the woman, and between thy seed and her seed: it shall bruise your head, and you shall bruise his heel.*

Genesis 3:15 has been long recognized as the first messianic prophecy of the Bible. It revealed three essential truths:

(1) Satan is the enemy of the human race, which explains why God put enmity which related to the word enemy between you [Satan] and the woman;

(2) He would place a spiritual barrier between her seed [Satan's] which related to people, and her seed, which is God's people; and

(3) The representative seed of the woman a human being: Christ would deliver the death-blow to Satan, but in so doing would be bruised himself.

It shall bruise "crush" your head, bruising of the heel refers to Christ's bruising on the cross, which led to the eventual crushing of Satan and his kingdom.

THE SORROW AND YOUR CONCEPTION:

The word sorrow means "birth pangs" and sounds like the Hebrew word for tree, which is a reminder of the source of this pain in the sin involving the tree of the knowledge of good and evil.

It also looks forward to the Crucifixion when the curse ultimately will be hung on a tree. Their desire has been variously interpreted.

(1) A physical desire s1trong enough to compensate for the pain of childbirth;

(2) Her natural desire to submit to her husband's leadership: or

(3) Perhaps a and I say perhaps because of not knowing for sure just going according to Scriptures by faith, so when I say her desire "against" her husband in not being willing to submit to him because of her fallen sinful nature.

Wives, submit yourselves unto your own husbands, as unto the Lord (Ephesians 5 :22).

This does not mean becoming a door mat. Christ at whose name *every knee shall bow, in heaven and on earth and under the earth* (Philippians 2: 1 0), submitted his will to the Father, and we honor Christ by following his example. When we submit to God, we become more willing to obey his commands to submit to others; that is, to subordinate our rights to theirs. In a marriage relationship, both husband and wife are called to submit.

- For the wife, this means willingly following her husband's leadership in Christ.
- For the husband, it means putting aside his own interests in order to care for his wife.

Submission is rarely a problem in a home where both partners have a strong relationship with Christ and where each is concerned for the happiness of the other.

****

A PRAYER OF THANKS

Lord, some days I feel weighted down by the routine. Help me now to rejoice in your presence. *God is our refuge and strength, a very present help in trouble* (Ps. 46:1). Father, thank you for your presence. *The Lord is nigh unto them that are of a Broken heart; and save such as be of a contrite spirit* (Ps. 34:18). Father I just want to say thanks for all you have done for me and being with me through your word, and for these whom you would have to read your word, bless and keep them as only you can Amen.

THE WISDOM OF GOD'S HOLY WORD

PRAYING CHRISTS' PRAYER AGENDA

JOHN 17:20-21

Neither pray I for these alone, but for them also which shall believe on me through their word; that they all may be one; as you Father, are in me, and I in you, that they also may be one in us: that the world may believe that you have sent me.

****

Printed in the United States
By Bookmasters